Aspects of moder sociology

SOCIAL RESEARCH

GENERAL EDITOR:
Maurice Craft
Foundation Dean of Humanities and Social Science,
The Hong Kong University of Science and Technology

ASPECTS OF MODERN SOCIOLOGY

General Editor:

Maurice Craft Foundation Dean of Humanities and Social Science,
The Hong Kong University of Science and Technology

SOCIAL RESEARCH

The limitations of social research
Prof. M. D. Shipman
Roehampton Institute of
Higher Education

Data collection in context
Stephen Ackroyd
and
John Hughes
University of Lancaster

Reading ethnographic research
Martyn Hammersley
The Open University

Ethics in social research
Dr. Roger Homan
Brighton Polytechnic

The philosophy of social research
John Hughes
University of Lancaster

The limitations of social research

MARTEN SHIPMAN B.SC. (SOC), PH.D.

Third Edition

Longman London and New York

Longman Group Limited,
Longman House, Burnt Mill, Harlow,
Essex CM20 2JE, England
and Associated Companies throughout the world.

Published in the United States of America
by Longman Publishing, New York

© Longman Group UK Limited 1973, 1981, 1988

First published 1973
Second edition 1981
Third edition 1988
Second impression 1995

British Library Cataloguing in Publication Data
Shipman, M. D.
   The limitations of social research. ——
   3rd ed. —— (Aspects of modern sociology.
   Social research).
   1. Social sciences —— Research
   I. Title   II. Series
   300'.72   H62
   ISBN 0-582-29729-X

Library of Congress Cataloging in Publication Data
Shipman, M. D.
   The limitations of social research.

   (Aspects of modern sociology.   Social research)
   Bibliography: p.
   Includes index.
   1. Social sciences——Research. I. Title. II. Series.
   H62.S464   1988   300'.72   87-3868
   ISBN 0-582-29729-X

Set in AM Comp/Edit 10/12pt Plantin

Produced through Longman Malaysia, PP

Contents

Editors' Preface   vii
Foreword   viii

PART ONE: Social research and science   1
Controversy 1: The nature-nurture dispute   1
1   Scientific activity in practice and in theory   5

Controversy 2: Do schools have any impact?   15
2   Social Science   19

Controversy 3: What really went on under the banyan trees?   32
3   Interpretive social science   37

PART TWO: Techniques for collecting information   47
Controversy 4: Has comprehensive schooling raised or lowered standards in Education?   48
4   Sampling   52

Controversy 5: Terrorist or resistance fighter? The case of the football hooligan   64
5   Studies based on observation   68

Controversy 6: What do school leavers think about schools?   74
6   Information through asking questions   78

Controversy 7: To stream or unstream?   90
7   Experiments   94

Controversy 8: When was childhood discovered?   102
8   Documents, unobtrusive measures and triangulation   107

PART THREE: The personal and political influences on research 117

Controversy 9: How could Psychology include fraud? The case of Sir Cyril Burt 119

9 The author, the date and the context 122

Controversy 10: The Swann Report and the politics of research 137

10 The publication of research 139

Controversy 11: Do teaching styles affect pupil progress? 155

11 The scope and limitations of social research 161

References and further reading 177
Index 193

Editors' Preface

The first series in Longman's *Aspects of Modern Sociology* library was concerned with the social structure of modern Britain, and was intended for students following professional and other courses in universities, polytechnics, colleges of education, and elsewhere in further and higher education, as well as for those members of a wider public wishing to pursue an interest in the nature and structure of British society.

This further series sets out to examine the history, aims, techniques and limitations of social research, and it is hoped that it will be of interest to the same readership. It will seek to offer an informative but not uncritical introduction to some of the methodologies of social science.

John Barron Mays
Maurice Craft

Foreword

The revisions to the third edition have been radical, reflecting changes in social science, and approaches to research and in its use. The image of the social researcher when the first edition was written was of a surveyor accumulating evidence from schools and other institutions by interview or questionnaire, but not interested in what went on inside them. Fifteen years later the image is of the researcher squatting as inconspicuously as possible in the Wendy House of an infant classroom. Behind those contrasting images lies a dramatic change in the perceived limitations of social science. These limits have been highlighted not only by attacks on the distortions resulting from the application of quantitative methods developed in the natural sciences, but by the exposure within social research itself that evidence might be sexist, racist and focused on the poor.

These changes have increased the importance of informing the scepticism that is essential in interpreting social research. The book remains a guide to the majority on the assessment of the credibility of published research. It is addressed first to students of social science, second to those (particularly in education) who use evidence from research, and third, to the public who meet this evidence through the media. Part 1 looks at the assumptions behind research, Part 2 looks at the methods used, and Part 3 looks at the way evidence is made public and incorporated into action. This is not just serious and technical. Although it is very important to inform those who use evidence from social research, the account covers the funny and the fraudulent.

Each chapter is preceded by a controversy selected from education. These illustrate the difficulties in using available evidence. The political nature of the debates within the education service have intensified these controversies since the first edition of the book. But they have also emphasised the intimate relation of research and the evidence produced, to the models of human behaviour and organisation that guided the researcher. That is probably the major revision in the third edition. It has become more important to inform users of social research about its scope and limitations. But this can only be done by showing how the world was modelled by the researcher in advance of designing the work and presenting the evidence.

The one unrevised part of the book is the three questions that should be asked of all research, quantitative and qualitative, scientistic and interpretive. The only exception is research intentionally designed to change and not just study, that is polemic rather than detached. That is the reason for also asking Question 4.

Key Question 1

If the investigation had been carried out again, by different researchers, using the same methods, would the same results have been obtained? The concern here is with the RELIABILITY of the methods used. This includes not only the way information has been collected, but the dependability of the researcher and the response of those studied. Social research involves interaction between scheming researchers and thinking subjects. There is never complete reliability because that interaction can never be fully controlled. If it were, the situation would no longer reflect reality.

Key Question 2

Does the evidence reflect the reality under investigation? The concern here is with the VALIDITY of the results obtained. Different researchers might obtain similar results using the same methods, but this reliability might still conceal a failure to obtain and present evidence that is a true reflection of the subject under investigation. Consistent results might still be far from the complexity and subtlety of human affairs. Because of this complexity, the human condition has to be modelled before it can be simplified and defined for investigation. Implicitly or explicitly these models are the source of hypotheses about behaviour and the bases for interpreting the evidence collected. That evidence has meaning in relation to the models used. Yet these may contrast sharply with those held by the reader. Thus, the score on an intelligence or reading test might be valid for the researcher, yet be a grossly over-simplified and invalid reflection of intellect or reading in all its aspects to the reader.

Key Question 3

What relevance do the results have beyond the situation investigated? The concern here is with the extent to which results can be generalised. Samples may be unrepresentative. Individuals under observation may not behave naturally. Results obtained here may not be applicable there. The past may be no guide to the future. Humans are marked by their variety. Generalisation from one to another may be misleading.

Key Question 4

Is there sufficient detail on the way the evidence was produced for the credibility of the research to be assessed? None of the three questions above can be answered unless the researcher provides sufficient information on the methods used and on the justification for their use. If the evidence is claimed to be based in research, the methods should be open to readers. That is the responsibility of the researcher and any work reported without the details necessary to ask the questions is suspect. Nor should exceptions be made as long as the label 'research' is used. Interpretive, observational research needs more, not less, emphasis on the methods used, because there is no established, traditional way of organising and reporting the work. Quantitative, statistical research results can be checked back to the methods used. Accounts from ethnography can only be distinguished from opinion if there is a methods section.

Many social scientists will reject this emphasis on displaying methods because it is scientistic, derived from the natural sciences. That is accepted, but the common distinction between quantitative and qualitative does not divide scientific from non-scientific approaches to the collection of evidence. Both come under the umbrella of social science. The important dividing line is between both of these scientistic approaches, and that which rejects detachment for involvement and sees the purpose of social science as polemic, as political, as revolutionary, concerned with changing not studying situations. Here it is the responsibility of the researcher to spell out that polemic purpose and not to maintain the appearance of doing research while rejecting the discipline that this involves, including making rationale and methods public.

It is the importance of research as a direct and indirect influence on public affairs which accounts for the balance of the book and its emphasis on the usually neglected aspects of theorising before, and presentation after, data collection. This also adds spice to an often technical and boring subject. Social research is important and is influential. But it is also fun for those involved and should not bore those who read it. When research meets human ingenuity and unpredictability it should reflect not conceal the variety.

M. D. SHIPMAN

PART *1* SOCIAL RESEARCH SCIENCE

CONTROVERSY *1*

THE NATURE-NURTURE DISPUTE

The Controversies that introduce chapters in this book have been selected because they reflect on crucial issues in the use of research evidence in education. This subject rests on the social sciences. These add the academic rigour to the initial and in-service education of teachers and inform policy, whether formulated in classroom, staff meeting, county or town hall, or the Department of Education and Science (D.E.S.). Yet in the most basic of educational issues there is controversy over the status of evidence. Academics argue over the factors that contribute to effective school organisation, to effective teaching and to effective classroom management. Even more basically, they disagree over the relative contributions of nature and nurture, of inheritance and environment, biology and culture to human attainments. Furthermore, that disagreement, stretching back over a century, shows how political as much as scientific influence determines what is investigated, what evidence is produced, and how it is interpreted.

Uncovering the factors behind human intelligence, attainment and personality is fundamental to improving effectiveness in education. A sociologist may concentrate on the social impact of background factors on the attainment of children, and in doing so is assuming that inheritance can be discounted. A psychologist comparing the attainments of fraternal and identical twins, some reared together and some apart is assuming that inheritance is going to be influential. A teacher deciding on work for her class will tailor it to the assumed characteristics of individual children and in doing so take into account factors assumed to lie in both inheritance or environment. Explicitly or implicitly this is an important question.

As the grip of religion, of custom, of the divine right of kings was lifted, biologists increasingly questioned the origins of life and its development. Darwin published *The Origin of Species* in 1859. Humanity came to be seen as governed by the same laws of natural selection as other animals. A powerful wing of biology, largely developed by Galton on the basis of study of twins, supported the 'vastly preponderating effects of nature over nurture'.[1]

In the early twentieth century social biology was dominated by hereditarians. In the nature–nurture dispute, the former was seen to be paramount. This also affected psychology. Thus McDougall's *An Introduction to Social Psychology* was published in 1908, listed instincts, blind impulses only slightly modifiable by learning as the driving force behind behaviour.[2] They were the prime movers of all human activity. There was an instinct to explain all important actions. The instinct for pugnacity explained why we were aggressive. The instinct of curiosity explained the quest to explore. Instincts of fear, flight, self-assertion, reproduction, acquisition and so on formed a comprehensive explanation for human behaviour. Neither was this book of short-lived influence. It was still a set text in the Post-Graduate Certificate of Education course at London University in the 1950s. A 31st edition appeared in 1960 and was reprinted in 1963. Lecturers take a long time to remove redundant books from recommended reading.

More sinister, the importance given to heredity and to natural selection led to the eugenics movement.[3] This started as a mission by scientists such as Galton and Pearson to improve the quality of the population. It was built up as an experimental and evangelical force until embraced by Hitler's Germany in a Eugenics Sterilisation Law in 1933 and the 'final solution' of the Jewish problem that followed. For three decades scientists had confidently used their knowledge of inheritance to press for the salvation of humanity through a eugenic programme. By 1930 that scientific base was in ruins and the reform programme had been taken over by thugs.

The opponents within biology to the views of the eugenicists were largely ignored in the 1920s and 1930s. The counter-attack came from the cultural anthropologists. As evidence accumulated that in small-scale societies there were exceptions to every inexorable law governing human behaviour promulgated by western biologists, the importance of learning, of nurture was increasingly apparent. In Controversy 3 the contribution of Margaret Mead is discussed. The technical flaws in her work are however of less importance than the way biological determinism was countered by anthropologists and by sociologists taking an extreme environmentalist view. The counter-attack was understandable. Davenport, the director of the Eugenics Record Office established in 1910, took the simple view that criminals and other deviants lacked the genes necessary for normal living. Making sure that they did not breed was a quick way to improve the human lot. This was countered by anthropologists such as Boas and Mead who maintained that behaviour was determined by learning from the culture. Criminality and other behaviours could be remedied through re-education. Both sides in the nature–nurture dispute took polarised positions. Neither made much allowance for human individuality and resilience. Both were deterministic.

The absurdity in these extreme views is clear fifty years later. It has now become politically sensitive even to consider biological differences in research on race or gender. Yet it is likely that the variation in every human characteristic is both genetic and learned. Biological determinism and cultural determinism are equally misleading. Furthermore, this has important implications for social policy. For example, if we manage to provide increased equality of educational opportunity, the importance of genetic variations will be increased. The policy would consolidate inequality of outcomes. In practice, nature and nurture interact and in the explanation of human characteristics, are inseparable.[4]

The reluctance to abandon the view that inheritance was of paramount importance in determining human characteristics can be seen in the efforts of Burt, late in his life, to defend the view that intelligence was largely inherited. There is little doubt that he resorted to fraud (see Controversy 9). Even more alarming was his power within educational psychology in England to suppress criticism of his views. It is the silence of the psychologists that has to be explained rather than the indiscretions of an old man. Similarly it is the ease with which biologists slipped from seeing the influence of inheritance of individuals to generalising about women or about races that serves as a warning about the application of scientific theories.

By the 1980s the pendulum had swung to the cultural

determinists. In practical terms this was fortunate, for it means that responsibility for learning can be placed with teachers, responsibility for a child's wellbeing with parents, welfare with social workers and so on. But there is a price to pay in this stress on environmental factors and the relegation of genetic factors. Teachers, parents, social workers and others have to shoulder full responsibility for failure. When nurture is king you cannot blame nature. The saying that 'there are no problem children, only problem parents' is fine for those who do not have the problems. It must have caused heartache in many caring yet troubled families.

This Controversy introduces many of the themes of this book. First, it shows how scientists work within models of the world that guide their perception of it. This accounts, not only for the way science can be used to support conflicting views, but how the evidence can change so dramatically generation after generation. Second, it illustrates the way political views percolate into scientific activity. The basis of socialism is a belief that the social and economic environment can be improved and hence that humanity will become healthier, wiser and peaceful. Conservatives tend to look to institutions that can cope with the imperfections of humanity. Part 3 is concerned with the way these views affect the publication of evidence. Third, the methods used in social research, covered in the central chapters of this book, tend to produce contradictions rather than agreement. The nature–nurture controversy lies behind Controversies 3, 9 and 10 where social and natural science overlap and where technical debate is mixed with skulduggery.

1

SCIENTIFIC ACTIVITY IN PRACTICE AND IN THEORY

Controversy 1 illustrated many of the limitations of research into human organisation and behaviour. First, the switch, within this century, from seeing humans as governed by instincts, programmed by inheritance, to seeing them as formed by their environments is a warning that dogmatism is misplaced. Both views tend to be rejected today. Secondly, the nature–nurture controversy shows how scientists can become blinkered within their models of the world, unable to distance themselves and even resorting to fraud to support their views. Third, the instinct-driven or the culturally-determined human seems a long way from the individual and often odd people around us. Humanity seems to have been depersonalised, automatised by the models used.

Natural as well as social scientists depend on simplifying complex reality. This process of simplification does not clearly distinguish scientific observation from everyday perception. When a pupil, or teacher, or parent meet a problem in education, they use a common-sense network of classifications, relations, causes and effects that enable the issue to be interpreted. Often metaphors are used to make sense of the unfamiliar by employing the familiar. Education is seen as an organism, growing, needing nourishment, inter-related or as a building, in danger of collapse needing shoring up or refurbishing. Scientific enquiry similarly involves the imaginative use of metaphors, the building of networks of explanations.[1] The scientific networks are labelled theories which help explain the world. Within science, networks that guide perception are not only shared but are taught, examined, often subjected to repeated experimentation, articulated by discussion, elaborated in books and papers and above all, exposed to the scrutiny of peers in the scientific community.

This view denies scientists a detached, objective stance. That is central to modern physics. Cottrell, a physicist, points to the development of atomic theory in the nineteenth century as the watershed in natural science.[2] Quantum mechanics and atomic theory suggested that when electrons, atoms or minute particles or waves were investigated, the object was itself disturbed during the act of observation. The world of the physicist became undetermined. Cause and effect were suddenly confused and the metaphor of the machine was seen as unsuitable.

This view of science does not deny its successes. Indeed, it celebrates it as a remarkable human achievement rather than the mechanical imposition of standard procedures. It is the adoption of the latter view that harmed the social sciences. Positivism, the application of the methods of the natural sciences to the study of humanity, may still have been beneficial had this method been seen as striving for objectivity rather than applying mechanistic procedures that ensured it. The latter degenerated into scientism where only experimental, quantitative methods were seen to lead to reliability and validity. Yet most of the important breakthroughs in natural science have come from extending existing knowledge, through using new metaphors, by implying comparisons between events and prior events, or treating associations as if they were the same as prior or parallel associations. Thus, Dalton formulated the atomic theory of gases at the start of the nineteenth century by treating gases, liquids and solids as if they were little solid balls where like repelled like, a view carried over from his earlier work on meteorology. Such metaphors abound in social science, from the metaphors of body politics, national wills and collective consciences, through education systems and cycles of deprivation to the human brain as a feedback loop or information processor.

Dalton's atomic theory involved the application of a simple idea used to examine the formation of rain, to the way gases were combined from different atoms. At first it was contentious. But by the end of the nineteenth century it had become a taken-for-granted model, institutionalised within the community of chemists. That is the sequence through which metaphors become models and the revolutionary becomes commonplace. The process starts with imagination and the acceptance by an at first reluctant scientific community, who finally defend it as legitimated wisdom.

It may take time, but new theories are accepted. Scientists may be blinkered within their models of the world. This book is full of examples where this led them to seeing things that were not there and refusing to accept others that were. Science has its priests and its mysteries. It may take revolution to get the new accepted. But the combination of theorising and observing, the potential rewards for the innovator and the practical harm that can result from ignoring new developments, put a time limit on resistance to change.

Thus, science is encouraged for its potential to improve the wealth of nations, to make nations strong and improve the human lot. From the award of Nobel or Lenin prizes at one end to the pressure to secure 'Science 5 to 16' in schools at the other, it has become a focus for investment. We pay £360,000 a year to belong to the European Incoherent Scatter Facility situated in the Arctic Circle and £35 million to play our part in smashing particles in C.E.R.N. Science is an accolade. One of Sir Keith Joseph's nastier blows was to remove the word 'Science' from the Social Science Research Council (S.S.R.C.) and rename it the Economic and Social Research Council (E.S.R.C.).

There are two approaches to a definition of science. One describes what scientists seem to be doing. The other prescribes what they should be doing. Both description and prescription oversimplify. Within each there are disagreements. There is no uniform scientific method. But there are assumptions and procedures that allow the questions about reliability, validity and generalisability to be asked. Beyond that there is controversy among those looking descriptively or philosophically upon scientists at work.

Scientists at work

There are a number of assumptions that are seen to lie behind the work of scientists. First, they are concerned with the material world. This is assumed to be real and open to investigation through the senses. The methods used are empirical, whereby knowledge is accumulated through observation. Thus natural scientists are not usually concerned with ideas or ideals but with relations among the material world they observe.

Secondly, science is often concerned with routine and repetition and this increases the confidence in the reliability of methods. Science is advanced by a combination of insight and observation. These activities are focused on the similarities and associations among the things observed, leading to their classification. This process is continuous. Classifications are themselves associated and other associations are predicted. This is not just induction, deriving general principles from observed instances, but active, insightful and deductive.

The product of this combination of observation, classifying and creative inference is often a model of the aspect of the material world being studied. This is a framework of associated factors from which hypotheses can be derived about further relationships. Thus, there is an inseparable relation between the models and the methods used in a science. Models are developed as ways of classifying and understanding events and then serve to generate hypotheses to be tested and ways of doing the testing. They are not exact representations of reality but selections of related classes of events. Thus they are simplified and economical, enabling scientists to reach understandings and establish connections between events. The cost of this simplification is in excluding other possible classifications of events and hence models of them. That means that other interpretations are always possible. The models are central to understanding science at any one time, in any one tradition, because they determine the perceptions of the scientists involved.

Consequently, the assumption is that scientists operate within communities that direct attention and activities to specific models and methods. The organisation of these communities imposes discipline on its members. This is clearly visible in the training, qualification and promotion of scientists. The training is long, due not only to the insistence on appropriate scientific A levels, but to the convention that research should follow a doctoral or Master's programme. Examination, particularly for a higher degree, is by senior academics. When the ambitious want to publish, their articles are referred by the same academics. The same guardians of the discipline serve on interview panels and provide references. Those who succeed have to satisfy the Great and Good that they have mastered the theories and methods of the craft and, at higher degree level, are observing their subject matter through the networks and models of the discipline.

There is an important consequence of the involvement of scientists in disciplined communities. It ensures that individuals have some protection from excessive outside pressure. They can work on issues seen as central in the community. They can cooperate on problems that are known to be soluble. They submit their evidence to the authorities in the community in a public fashion, through publication. The arbiter of the validity of evidence is the community itself. That community is often spread around the world. There is danger in this process of public, communal validation. It exposes the new to the authority of the established. If the community is itself politically penetrated or stuck with a tottering set of models, innovation will be inhibited. Shared models ensure cumulative effort but can shut alternative explanations and avenues for research.

To avoid complacency therefore, return to the end of the nineteenth century. It was a critical time for science for suddenly new explanatory networks were needed to explain the phenomena of radioactivity, and atoms. Quantum Theory, Relativity, the Uncertainty Principle were efforts to explain this new world of nature. They were leaps of imagination showing object and subject as inseparable. One development of this time, the discovery of X-rays by Röntgen in 1895 was particularly exciting. Solids were suddenly observed to be full of holes, for X-rays passed through them like light through glass. Scientists were alerted to the probability that rays of other frequencies would be found through further experimentation.

In 1903, Blondlot announced the discovery of *n*-rays, which gave no photographic effect but could be detected through observing their effect on the luminosity of phosphorescent surfaces. The discovery was quickly confirmed by other French scientists, and by 1904, seventy-seven scientific publications had included descriptions of the applications of these rays, how to detect them, the materials that emitted them, their wavelength and spectrum. Yet outside France no one seemed to be able to detect *n*-rays through replicating Blondlot's work. In 1904, shortly after Blondlot had been awarded the Lalande prize for his discovery, the rays were shown to be the result of his faulty observations. The discovery of

X-rays by Röntgen in 1896 had led to a great interest in such phenomena, and Blondlot and others were too ready to be convinced by their own fallible perception. After 1909 the *n*-ray passed out of science, its discoverer having gone mad. Poor Professor Rene or Prosper or plain M Blondlot, Blondot or Blandot: even in death he is not respected, for these three versions of his name appeared in the three references cited here.[3]

Blondlot was a victim of his own expectations, an extreme, unfortunate but understandable occurrence given the way scientists go about their work. Yet the deception of science publicised as the impinging of facts on an open mind followed by induction to derive theories from this evidence is built into every scientific paper. Medawar has argued that the scientific paper is a fraud because it suggests observation and experiment followed by discussion of the results obtained.[4] But that is to reverse the actual process which starts with the expectations built into models that guide the observations made and their interpretation. The scientist selects THE problem, designs THE research and analyses THE results by reference to existing theory. The key stage in research, the formulation of hypotheses, consists of hunches derived in this way. Science is normally problem solving, not a thrust into the unknown.

Medawar is drawing a distinction between two parts of scientific research. There is the inspiration, creation, imagination and guesswork that finally leads to a hypothesis. There is then deduction from this hunch, followed by a second stage that can be a rigorous process of testing of the ideas. Both come from within the same discipline. But the real sequence of scientific research is inspiration then observation, not observation then inspiration as implied in streamlined written papers. Normal science consists of problem solving with the results anticipated because they will fit into the existing jigsaw. The imaginative stage occurs as the problem is first defined. As the data are collected they impinge on a mind already anticipating it. The scientific paper reverses the real sequence in order to preseve the impression of science as an inductive activity.

The scientific paper is part of the mystery of science, preserved as in other professions to exclude the bogus but also to bolster authority in relation to the public. The Latin Mass, the doctor's illegible prescription, the dentist's white coat and the social scientist's jargon all serve the same purposes. Communities maintain internal discipline and defend their boundaries by traditions that may have little practical but much symbolic value. Science is popularly seen as inductive, as deriving general laws from empirical activity, and it does no harm to defend that image particularly as it is the basis for passing examinations, obtaining a higher degree, getting work published and, above all, attracting funds for research from a public who still see science as the objective collection of data. But it remains a fraud.

The conclusion from this review of scientists at work is that they operate within shared assumptions about the world they study. These assumptions structure their perceptions. They are often metaphorical, drawing on models from often unrelated areas. This view of science puts theories, models, conceptual frameworks, paradigms, networks of classifications at the centre. These terms all express the same idea. Scientists model the world in order to make sense of its complexities. These models enable them to build on existing evidence, to hypothesise about what is yet to be found. There is disagreement over science as an activity aimed at disproving existing models or confirming them and over the power of models to blinker their adherents. But scientists at work are no longer seen as unrestrained observers. They are disciplined by shared models developed within communities that determine what is accepted as valid evidence.

Philosophical views of science

Three philosophical views of science can be distinguished. First, there are those who have held that science is indeed concerned with the collection and interpretation of raw data impinging on an open mind. Second, there are more recent approaches that incorporate the idea of a scientific community influencing members and sharing conceptual frameworks that influence observation and interpretation. But here there is a necessary further division between those such as Popper who see scientific activity as critical and rational,[5] and those like Kuhn who see it as organised to preserve agreement, often ignoring cases that don't fit established ideas.[6]

The classical view of science was inductive. Scientists were supposed to observe or experiment with an open mind and to produce general laws from the data collected. Science was liberated from religion, magic and superstition. The scientist was the enlightened man, objective, detached, and following where his senses took him as he looked into natural or social events. Observation was seen as leading to classification and hence to further empirical experimentation until laws could be stated.

The weakness of this classical, inductive view of science has already been illustrated. Data are not observed raw, but cooked by expectations fostered amid a scientific community sharing models that direct observation and interpretation. The scientific mind is no more an empty bucket into which observations pour than are the minds of non-scientists. Popper, writing in Vienna between the wars, was concerned with the demarcation between science and non-sciences such as religion and magic. Three features distinguish science. First, statements that cannot be falsified are not scientific. Hence on this definition most social research is not science. Sir Keith Joseph's knowledge of Popper's writing put paid to 'science' in the title SSRC. Second, science is both rational and critical, a search for the case where the hypothesis does work out. Third, it assumes a scientific mind already loaded with theories, networks, models before engaging in observation and hence of science, not as an individual but as a collective exercise. Behind the theories that guide the observations is a scientific community supporting the direction of the empirical work.

Popper's *The Logic of Scientific Discovery* prescribes scientific activity.[7] Its importance was in rejecting the view that the scientific sequence was the collection of raw data through an open mind followed by theorising to establish relations. To Popper the reverse was to happen, theorising preceded the selection of data. The action started with theory not observation. But Popper's assumption of science as collective and swingeingly critical in the attempt to falsify, does not measure up with much of the normal activities of scientists. The history of science and the study of the way scientists are trained and work together suggests that the thrust to falsify is rare. Normal science consists rather of the attempt to confirm.

Kuhn's *The Structure of Scientific Revolutions* was published in 1962.[8] It traces the history of science and throughout stresses that it is the authority of established scientists that determines the status of evidence. On Kuhn's view the scientific community becomes an influence for limiting criticism of established theory, not a support for trying to falsify it. Normal science to Kuhn consisted of working within a 'paradigm', a framework of meanings and procedures that were taken for granted. These determined the selection of data and their interpretation, and both were directed towards filling indentified gaps in the paradigm. Normal science was not critical but confirmatory. It was productive because it focused on soluble puzzles within the paradigm. Only in occasional revolutions were scientific communities shifted from their entrenched paradigms.

Popper's hard line of refutation as the aim, or Kuhn's softer line of normal science as confirmation are not reconcilable. Neither are directly applicable to social science, where human ingenuity creates exceptions to every law and where the disciplines are too young to have established paradigms. Here there is a vast audience for the speculative. Students can still find that their higher degree theses are published and influential. In the natural sciences research is more a collective activity, more expensive and less likely to overturn existing models. Here scientists do tend to concentrate on the soluble, to have strong expectations of the continuity of new developments and to be wary of the novel.

At the turn of the century Simon Newcomb was a professor of mathematics and astronomy at Johns Hopkins University, a founder and first president of the American Astronomical Society, and vice-president of the National Academy of Sciences. Among many papers he had published was one that anticipated Einstein's special theory of relativity. By analysing the relation between weight and lift he concluded, in an article titled 'The Outlook for the Flying Machine', that 'The mathematician of today admits that he can neither square the circle, duplicate the cube or trisect the angle. May not our mechanicians, in like manner, be ultimately forced to admit that aerial flight is one of the great class of problems with which man can never cope, and give up all attempts to grapple with it'.[9] This article appeared on 22 October 1903. On 17 December 1903 the Wright brothers flew their powered machine. Even three years later Newcomb was still writing that it was demonstrated that powered flight was not possible. The problem was that the Wright brothers received little publicity. The first eyewitness account to be published only appeared in 1905. It may not have been believed. It is more likely not to have been read. It appeared in the January issue of *Gleanings in Bee Culture*. [10]

DO SCHOOLS HAVE ANY IMPACT?

With over £15,000,000,000 being spent on the education service each year it seems odd to ask whether schools are effective. Yet the evidence is not clear. Once the social background of the children and their achievements at intake are taken into account, there is no incontrovertible evidence that the way schools are organised or children taught makes any difference. In an expensive service in which a lot of people claim to be experts in training, inspecting and advising on the organisation of learning it's a depressing situation. Read an H.M.I. report, a book on how to teach or a politician talking about comprehensive schooling and confidence oozes. Read the research and there is disagreement over whether the organisa-tion of learning matters at all. This applies to the USA as well as the UK. A Rand Corporation review of available evidence concluded that 'Research has not identified a variant of the educational system that is consistently related to students' educational outcomes'.[1] In this controversy we are near the theoretical and technical difficulties that define the limitations of social research.

There is a difficulty in reviewing the evidence on school effects. Is the problem in detecting them due to the ineffectiveness of schools, or inadequacies in the research? When the evidence is reviewed, the latter becomes suspect. Large-scale studies tend to show no school effects. Coleman from a study of 4,000 schools concluded that they had little influence on the attainment of their children.[2] Yet small-scale studies often show large effects. The reason is in the factors taken into account. Large-scale statistical studies such as Coleman or Jencks[3] have to depend on quantifiable attainment and organisational measures. But examination results or standardised test scores are a restricted reflection of the objectives of schooling. Even more restricted is the dependence on quantitative measures of the processes in schools. Many of the most important aspects of teaching and learning may be in the realm of attitudes and relationships and not open to statistical calculation or even observation.

Small-scale studies yield richer data on these process factors. Thus, Rutter *et al.* with twelve schools,[4] Reynolds with nine[5] and Mortimore *et al.* with fifty,[6] not only conclude that good and bad schools can be distinguished, but that the factors producing the contrast can be identified. These factors are little to do with formal school organisation, resources or class sizes which are easily measured, and a lot to do with school culture or ethos, leadership, expectations and involvement which can often only be inferred. Significantly this brings researchers very close to inspectors, advisers and teachers who also see the crucial factors in school effectiveness in these inter-personal factors that are beyond direct measurement or evaluation.

The publication of *Fifteen Thousand Hours* in 1979 produced a classical critical response.[7] It was immediately welcomed by local education authorities for uncovering the factors behind successful schooling. At last researchers had shown what distinguished good from poor schools. The importance of school ethos and contributing factors such as the setting and checking of homework, punctuality in starting lessons and running the school as a 'tight ship' were built into in-service training and guidance from H.M.I. But the academic community took the book apart as it had Bennett's *Teaching Styles and Pupil Progress* in 1976 (see Controversy 11).

There is a wealth of critical attack and spirited counter-attack on *Fifteen Thousand Hours*, all tributes to its importance. There are two collections of essays,[8] each with a response by the Rutter team, attacks by the professional hatchet men of educational research,[9] some equally matched attacks and counter-attacks, and a review of the criticisms.[10] These disputes will never be resolved because the confidentiality given to the twelve schools involved means that all the data can never be opened to further analysis. But the contrast between the acceptance of the results by education authorities and the attacks on it by the research community was astonishing.

The criticisms of *Fifteen Thousand Hours* ranged across reliability, validity and generalisability. Goldstein concluded that the results

should be treated with caution if not scepticism.[11] There were
problems over the very limited control over the intake characteristics of the children which could have accounted for the
differences in output and results not statistically significant were
unjustifiably dismissed as unimportant. The study related many
process variables with the output measures of attendance,
delinquency, examination results and behaviour, but not so that
their interrelation could be shown to account for the attainments of
particular children. Critics found no satisfactory basis for the
emphasis put on school ethos, saw correlations being confused with
causes, criticised the statistical analyses and deplored the neglect of
social class and other powerful factors that influence attainment.
The schools were not only few in number but seen as untypical in
their location and level of resourcing.[12]

This catalogue of criticisms didn't disturb the influence of
Fifteen Thousand Hours nor inhibit its authors in defending it.
Mortimore, one of the co-authors, continued with this style of
research to direct a study of primary school effectiveness.[13]

This controversy illustrates the close connection between the
conceptualisation of an issue and the design of research into it. The
crudest design takes a number of schools and compares some
indication of their outcomes such as examination results. But this
controversy shows how difficult it is to draw conclusions from such
comparisons. So a second research design sees the school in terms of
input–output. That may show differences between schools with
similar intakes, but gives no information to account for how they
came about. So the school is further conceptualised as input-
process-output. That is close to the Rutter *et al.* design. But other
factors around the school may still influence attainments within it,
so account is next taken of the context of the schools. This steady
elaboration of conceptualisation and design can be seen in
Mortimore *et al.'s* 1986 study of primary schools for the Inner
London Education Authority. This study is full of detail on what
goes on in the 50 schools studied and on the 2,000 children followed
through their primary schooling. Particular attention is paid to
problems identified by critics of Rutter and Bennett.[14] Its critical
reception is still to come at the time of writing.

There has also been an accumulation of large data bases on school
outcomes that will serve for detailed analyses from hereon. For

example, the Scottish Education Data Archive based on successive school leavers studied at the Centre for Educational Sociology at the University of Edinburgh has produced increasingly valuable analyses of the factors behind successful schooling.[15] The archive is now yielding data on the effectiveness of schools for particular categories of children.[16]

This work on school effects shows how the absence of adequate theory limits the scope of social research. Even taking contexts, inputs, processes and outputs into account, the models of schooling used are crude. We are a long way from specifying the factors in school organisation that are under our control and that can be changed to improve the education of particular groups of children. There is now evidence that there are differences in the effectiveness of different schools. But there is no detectable model of schooling unifying the studies. Consequently the work has not been cumulative even though later studies have learned from the criticisms of earlier work. Given the severity of the critics that is wise. But the lack of theory limits the value of the inheritance and means that there has been no testing of hypotheses derived from theoretical models of the school. Thus this work remains detached from the main body of social science concerned with schooling and learning. More factors will be built into future research and the statistical manipulation of the data will become more sophisticated. But only when there is a model of schooling will there be casual relations established that could be used with confidence.[17] That is not an academic hope, but a serious practical issue. It is the clue to finding out how schools influence children. Researchers are still uncovering the associations between individual input, process and output factors without any confidence that their total inter-relation is known. Yet teachers have to assume they know these inter-relations every hour of the school day.

2

SOCIAL SCIENCE

The claims for a science of society were established in the mid-nineteenth century. At this time the hopes were high, not only because science was uncovering the working of the natural world and enabling humans to control it, but because this scientific method was seen as free of mystery, superstition and religious obscurity. Human reason, applied through the systematic observation of events and the formulation of theories based on the data collected, was to be the mainspring of progress. To apply this scientific method to human behaviour and social organisation was an obvious next step.

By the end of the century, when natural science was having to adjust to an indeterminate, unpredictable atomic basis for the natural world and the world-as-a-machine metaphors were being abandoned, social science was engaged in a search for laws of human development and for forces that controlled behaviour. Yet humanity was even more unpredictable than the material world.

The legacy of this nineteenth century thinking still dominates much of social science. Three major influences survive. Darwin left a tradition of humanity evolving through natural selection, governed by genetic endowment. Marx postulated a predictable unrolling of history to an inevitable end, the classless society. Freud saw humanity driven by the id, lurking deep beyond the control of reason. All three saw humans as governed by forces beyond individual control whether in the genes, in history, or in the unconscious. Unfettered human reason had produced fettered models of the human condition.

It would be misleading however to neglect the positive contribution of the systematic theorising and data collection that lies at the heart of the attempt to make the study of humanity scientific. The dangers in formulating concepts and theories and then researching to test, illustrate or improve hypotheses is in distorting, diminishing human variety and ingenuity. It led to determinism wherein individuals were seen as at the mercy of forces beyond their control. The rejection of these is dealt with later. First the strength of this scientific approach, now often neglected, is outlined.

The beneficial legacy of trying to use the methods of the natural sciences in the study of human behaviour and organisation lies in the combination of model and method outlined in Chapter 1. Too many books on research list techniques of research as if they were neutral tools to be taken down and used when convenient. Once it is accepted that scientists approach issues with expectations of results based on models established in advance, theory and method, model and technique, are inseparable. Methods are selected because of the models held as well as the issue under review.

This sequence from theory to method and hence to evidence is often left out of accounts of research. The 'logy' in the methodology is neglected. It is usually left implicit in the designs of investigations. Yet the choice of method and its interpretation depend, implicitly or explicitly, on the theoretical models used.

In practice, the tricky steps in research design are in moving from concepts such as social class or alienation to indicators that can be used for collecting data. The former are abstract, embedded in theory. They have to be reduced to statements on an observation schedule, to items on a questionnaire, to indicators that reflect the concepts directly or indirectly. The original complexity and subtlety may be diminished by the need to depend on crude indicators. The graffiti on school walls may reflect the current state of adolescent morals or alienation from capitalist values, but could just be some lout having fun. Once data are collected this key process of linking theory and data is reversed. Now the answers to questions, observations and indicators have to be interpreted by reference back to the theory. Data from research are collected because they reflect implicit or explicit theory. They only become meaningful when interpreted against that theory.

This not only means that techniques are justified by reference to theories that inform the research as they guide the perceptions of the researchers, but that there are no such things as 'facts'. Things observed, measured, answered have no meaning until they are interpreted against the theory that guided the observation, measurement or survey. In Chapter 1 it was stressed that science was selective because of preconceptions held by communities of scientists. That is the reason why a movement such as Mass Observation fizzled out.[1] it attempted to observe and describe. But interpretation is inevitable. In science it is made explicit. You cannot claim to be both scientific and to observe unselectively.

In the social sciences researchers will approach their subjects with one or more models developed within one of many different disciplines. These models are simplifications of complex reality. Economists' models of the market do not include all the complications in supply or demand. Keynesian or monetarist models are the subject of academic and political dispute centred on their over-simplifications. Sociologists draw on metaphors of societies as organisms or systems as the subject of unrolling dialectical force generated by changing technology, or as negotiated networks of individual meanings. Psychologists model behaviour as stimulus and response or complex cognitive processing. In all disciplines there are mathematical modellers at one end and others putting humans at the centre of interest at the other. But econometricians, sociometricians, psychometricians, employing mathematical models for top-down application at one end, and social phenomenologists, social interactionists and ethogenicists keeping the whole person at the centre of research at the other, all model first, design their research with the model in mind, use methods that follow from the theoretical position and convert observations into meaningful data by reference to it.

This variety and the basing of research in often entrenched theoretical positions is why there is disagreement between and within disciplines. The social sciences are in their infancy as academic disciplines. Hence the models used change rapidly. In sociology, for example, the period to 1920 in the UK and USA was dominated by evolutionary theories and comparative studies of whole societies. From 1920 to the mid-1930s life histories and observational studies dominated in the USA based at the University of Chicago, while surveys exercised the few UK sociologists.[2] From the mid-1930s to the 1960s, survey and statistical methods took over only to be supplanted by interpretive methods once more in the 1970s. These changes were not produced by new techniques becoming available, but by new or revived views on the nature of human behaviour and organisation. Indeed, the fashion for qualitative, observational research came just as computers came into general use.

The youthful state of social research means that there is little of the routine problem-solving dominant in the established natural sciences. This is a joyous state, for research designs can be imaginative and results are unpredictable. Professor Humphreys of the University of Southern Illinois sets out to investigate the 'tearoom' trade.[3] This consists of homosexual activity in men's toilets. Now this is not easy to research, but Humphreys managed not only to observe 120 sexual acts in 19 different loos in 5 parks in his chosen city, but to complete 50 interviews from the 100 men observed to visit the 'tearooms'. This takes persistence, ingenuity as well as disregard for ethics. Pilot observations were carried out in toilets in New York, Chicago, St Louis, Kansas City, Des Moines, Tulsa, Denver, Los Angeles and San Francisco. To obtain the sample for interviewing, Humphreys took down the car numbers of visitors to his intensively studied 'tearooms' and then added the names identified to the list of a social health survey he was also engaged in. The surprise is that 50 per cent cooperated, although they may have felt under some compulsion to respond given his success in observing their earlier assignation.

The contribution of scientistic social science

The terms positivistic, empiricist and scientistic all sum up an approach to the study of humanity that sticks as close as possible to methods developed in the natural sciences. There are two key aspects that still dominate much of social science. First, the pre-specification of theories, and models, and the definition of the concepts involved. Second, the use of methods of collecting data that guarantee some reliability, particularly by controlling the views of the researcher. Most books on research methods emphasise these two bases for research. In practice they are often left implicit. One of the aims of this book is to help the reader search out the hidden models of human behaviour and organisation that lie behind evidence and to dig out the methods used.

The importance of systematic methods in social research has also been ignored in many of the attacks on scientistic approaches to the human lot. Yet these not only give some guarantee that there has been control over extraneous factors, including the researcher, but they enable critics to assess the credence of the evidence presented. That emphasis on methods is often tedious for the reader, but the discipline is a strength of science. Adopting conventional methods means accepting their discipline. Even more important it means that others can assess reliability. Indeed, if you are afraid of being hammered by critics, don't engage in quantitative research and spell out the methods used. It is safer to engage in observational case studies which are difficult to criticise because no standard methods need be adopted.

The contribution of the scientistic approach can be gauged from one tradition of research in the sociology of education. In 1926 Lindsay published a study relating education opportunity among the children of London to their social class.[4] The evidence of inequality and waste of talent was confirmed in 1938.[5] Since then there have been a series of studies confirming the inequality and injustice by relating social class and educational opportunity and achievement. Floud, Halsey and Martin,[6] Glass,[7] Douglas *et al*.,[8] Fogelman[9] and Halsey, Heath and Ridge[10] are the more prominent studies. The activity has decreased only because gender and racial injustice have been of more concern in the 1970s and 1980s. However, gender and racial injustice are closely related to social class position and the research tradition flourishes.[11]

It is difficult to over-emphasise the importance of reminding the public and policy-makers of the injustice within the education service. That is a major part of the strength of this tradition. It has been about important political issues. It relates education to the wider social and political structure. It is often convincing because the evidence has been confirmed through repeated research. That research has been exposed to critical treatment, facilitated by the use of methods that are open to criticism. The scientistic tradition ensured not only that a crucial social issue was kept on the political agenda for over sixty years, but that the evidence was convincing through its exposure to criticism. The scientistic tradition may treat humans as statistics and has led to determinism that further diminishes them. But it does deal with important issues and is open to the key activity of science as a reliable way of accumulating evidence, the scrutiny of methods by peers.

The move towards small-scale, interpretive social science

There have been four dangers in scientistic research on the human condition. First, there was the tendency, already discussed, for theories to be deterministic. Humans were seen as driven by forces beyond their control. Second, there was a related assumption that there were laws governing human behaviour. Yet a century of research has only uncovered a few minor, context-bound psychological hypotheses. These two dangers added up to dehumanisation, to people as puppets tugged about by forces applied by history, by culture, by institutions as if these were not the products of human action.

The third danger was that it was easy to construct a model of behaviour, or social change and then slide into assuming that it was real not constructed. The models were 'reified' given a concrete, even god-like status. The problem is that definition of all terms used is boring and would turn off any audience. Hence these are often used in a slipshod way. To refer to an education system is a useful shorthand. But this is a metaphor suggesting inter-related parts that serve a working whole. Terms like alienation, capitalism, the state, the establishment, are freely used yet ill-defined, extracted from the models that give them meaning. States, capitalism, social classes, schools, do not oppress or reward; this is done by individuals. The model is a short-hand often concealing the complexity of the real world. The social science tends to research top-down. It rarely probes the rich or powerful. The tendency is to examine the effectiveness of established organisations rather than looking for alternatives. Thus, in education the research into social class and educational opportunity was focussed on the shortcomings of the working of the organisation of schooling. It did not challenge that organisation but was aimed at improving its effectiveness. The problems tackled were 'taken', not 'made'.[12] They were the concerns of those in charge of education where what may have been needed was a new perspective from the viewpoint of those served by schools. The spotlight is usually on the deprived, not those who deprive them. By the 1980s the full extent to which social scientists had been blindfolded within their own models became apparent as blacks and women showed, from their perspectives, that social research had become white and male orientated.[13]

During the period when the social sciences were expanding rapidly, male views of the world were dominant even though a majority of undergraduates in subjects such as sociology were women. Only when women began to examine the social sciences they were practising did the bias become obvious. Women were invisible unless they were researched for their relation to men. The world was not merely seen through male eyes, but the norms were seen as masculine. Words such as 'he', 'Man', 'Mankind' were used not only for males but for all humans.

At the heart of this male-orientated social science were biological fallacies. Here the social inequalities of women were explained by reference to biological differences. These can be found in most anthropological studies examining, for example, the treatment of women during menstruation, pregnancy or childbirth. The behaviour was explained by reference to biology. But women have since reinterpreted this evidence so that the social behaviour is explained in social terms. Thus, primitive societies were usually seen as surrounding menstruating women with taboos. Sexual intercourse was forbidden and contacts restricted to avoid contamination through the menstrual blood. But these taboos can be reinterpreted as showing the power of women to deny men sexual intercourse at this time of the month and to voluntarily limit their power to bring calamity to men who touched them.

It has been argued recently that it is necessary to do feminine research to ensure that women become visible in social science. Anyone doubting that much research evidence has a male bias built into it should read *Doing Feminist Research*[13] or *Breaking Out: Feminist Consciousness and Feminist Research*[14] and look at re-interpretations by females of evidence originally produced by males. They should also remember that for over a century such evidence, now reinterpreted as male-centred, was never thought of as sexually biased. Then other groups, the Blacks, the poor, those with special needs, the aged and so on should be remembered for they also interpret and shape their lives in relation to others. At the heart of social research are assumptions that are open to challenge. This may have gone further in sociology than in psychology or economics, but all are open to the accusation of possibly unintended, but certainly identifiable bias, right in the framework of meanings where the enquiry begins.

The fourth danger in scientistic social research was to ignore the questing nature of humanity, forever trying to make sense of events. In the natural sciences only the scientist models the situation being studied. In the social sciences those studied also describe, analyse, give meaning to political, social, economic events and build up models of human behaviour in order to interact with others. It is the sharing of aspects of these common sense models which enables social life to proceed. But it presents the traditionally scientifically-minded researcher with a validity problem. Imposing pre-defined concepts through questions and categories involves violating just those responses which enable the respondent to make sense of the event being investigated.

This problem has been at the centre of a profound change in recent thinking about social research. Understanding the debate is central in answering questions about reliability and validity. The story starts with social science developing through the use not just of the methods of the natural sciences, but with the classical view of these as the objective observation of events, verification through repeated testing and finally the statement of universal laws. Today the view of science as the treatment of data through the use of pre-established theoretical models is seen as inappropriate for studying human behaviour because it imposes a straitjacket on the collection of the crucial data on how humans make their world intelligible. That means that the researcher must get to know the symbolic world of those studied not ignore it while concentrating on overt behaviour. Inner thoughts not appearances become the subject of study. The emphasis has shifted to uncovering the meanings given to the situations researched by those actually involved, and in their terms, not that of the researcher. The natural situation is presented in the enquiry. Social research tries to tell how those studied see things. Nothing could be farther from the natural sciences where the subjects studied can usually be assumed to lack an enquiring, interpreting mind.

An informative way of looking at the change in social research is to compare Durkheim's *Rules of Sociological Method*[15] first published at the turn of the century and Giddens' *New Rules of Sociological Method* published in 1976.[16] Giddens traces the changing philosophy of social science across the twentieth century, the progressive acceptance of the meaningful nature of human interaction and the need for social scientists to concentrate on the mutual knowledge, the frameworks of meaning used in that intercourse. He concludes with rules that are diametrically opposed to those recommended by Durkheim.

Durkheim was the inheritor of Comte's positivism. Across a whole century the insight in his work informed sociology. In *Suicide* in particular he used statistical data to analyse the way individuals appear to respond to social pressures to produce an extraordinarily powerful account of the way societies work.[17] In *The Rules of Sociological Method* he pressed for social facts to be treated as things, as external to the individual. The social world was constraining, moral, normative. The rules of research were to focus on the indicators of this constraint. These would very often be reflected in statistics of collective activity. The researcher was advised not to dwell on the reflecting, reflexive individual.

Gidden's *New Rules of Sociological Method* reverses Durkheim's emphasis. Now social relations and organisation are to be treated as skilled performances of individuals. Instead of remaining aloof as a detached observer, the rule is to get immersed in the action being studied. This is not just a blueprint for bottom-up research, but a reversal of the priorities within social science. Society is no longer seen as external and constraining, but as a network of meanings, subject to continuing change as individuals interact and interpret. This reversal is central to understanding the relation between research and theory. Once one changed, so did the other. Significantly the major influence among contemporary interpretive sociologists, G. H. Mead, worked at the University of Chicago where, from the 1920s on, sociologists were tramping the streets, the dance halls, the slums and the dosshouses recording behaviour and showing how those involved explained, informed and controlled their lives, however sordid.[18]

The switch to qualitative approaches now dominates the study of education as elsewhere.[19] It is an acknowledgement that the aim of a natural science of society has failed. The hopes of Comte in the nineteenth century that the application of science as then understood would strip away the mystery and reveal the working of social life as it had the natural world have been dashed. Science itself turned out to contain dogmas if not mystification, and in practice was inappropriate for studying the social world. More important, humans change their behaviour, alter their social relations, influence social organisation as part of everyday living. Society is an abstraction, and like any concept in social science should not be treated as a detached, unchanging, unproblematic entity. Societies, social classes, communities, schools and that group of children being observed by a researcher are being changed continually by those involved. They change the world around them because they have to act as if they understand it. They act as amateur social scientists in order to survive and hopefully prosper.

Several levels of model or meaning system or network can be distinguished in the loading of observation and interpretation in common sense and in social science. At base there are beliefs about the nature of life, its origins and direction that give some meaning to existence. Above these general beliefs are more specific notions of the supposed structure of society, some of which has been organised into models of the social world such as functionalism or Marxism in sociology, or behaviourism or cognitive science in psychology. But above that, everyone has some collection of meanings that enables the world to be interpreted, whether as a system, as a centre of conflict, or of the mind as responding to external stimuli or as a complex information-processing system. It is not just social scientists who differ over interpretations of social events. It is through the disagreements among people using common-sense meanings that behaviour and social organisation is changed. It is the acknowledgement of the similarity between social scientific models and those in everyday use that has changed the methodology of social research and brought the everyday meanings to the centre of enquiry.

Research in practice

When social research is examined in practice rather than in books on method, many of the academic distinctions about scientistic and interpretive approaches disappear. This is partly because the issue under investigation tends to dictate methods. You cannot question babies, usually have only limited opportunities to observe intimate sexual behaviour and are denied access to documents on the capital of the rich.

Visualise, for example, McCaghy and Skipper researching for their articles 'Lesbian behaviour as an adaptation to the occupation of stripping' and 'Striptease: the anatomy and career contingencies of a deviant occupation'.[20] The two sociology professors observe in clubs and burlesque theatres in ten cities from New York to Honolulu. Having watched the girls on stage they introduce themselves backstage as preparing an anthology on burlesque. They manage thirty-five interviews. There is also statistical comparison of the height, weight, bust and hip measurements of the sample with Playboy Playmates of the month and average American women. The need to adjust methods to the subject in social science can lead to some interesting empirical opportunities.

There is however a far more profound reason why the insulation between scientistic and interpretive methods is so porous. Despite many articles on their irreconcilable nature, it is a brave step to reject the natural scientific model and its apparently hard data. First, it is likely to lose you research funds, for the public and many senior academics still hold to a traditional view of science. Second, once you have been observing for a while, the need to interview systematically can become pressing. And once you have quantitative data it tends to be given priority, regardless of criticism of its distorting effects.

This use of 'hard' data as fact and 'soft' observational data as illustration is common. Thus Newby, having taken 'voluminous fieldwork notes' in his 1977 study of Suffolk farm workers nevertheless looks back with surprise at his book because it contains little on the participant observation and is mostly concerned with survey data.[21] Stierer makes a similar observation in reviewing Southgate et al's *Extending Beginning Reading*.[22] Here reading test scores are taken as the true measure against which teachers' assessments of children's reading is compared. Stierer justifiably asks why the tests, so heavily criticised, are still taken as the baseline and not themselves compared to teacher assessments to check test reliability and validity.

The grip of the scientistic view has not been released by a lot of writing about its weaknesses and the strength of interpretive, observational methods. It remains the public view of what social research should be about. It is still seen by most higher degree students as setting the criteria for assessing master's and doctoral theses and dissertations. It is still the basis for judging worth on promotion and appointment committees. We live with an image of research derived from the laboratory. The four key questions at the start of this book are derived from this approach. Until a convincing alternative definition of social research achieves widespread acceptance, those questions will be asked. Once they are jettisoned, investment in social science is likely to plummet.

The degree of control exercised distinguishes the top-down pre-categorised research of this chapter from the bottom-up, naturalistic research of the next. It also stretches designs along a spectrum. At one end is naturalistic, observational research usefully grouped together as ethnography where the objective is to let the interpretations of those being studied emerge without distortion from the design of the work. At the other extreme is laboratory experiment where control is rigorous to exclude any influence from factors extraneous to the hypothesis being tested. In between are types of social survey in which the categories used are carefully defined to ensure reliability but where the control of extraneous variables is left to statistical manipulation of the data collected, a procedure dependent on the sampling used and the subject of Chapter 4. This crude spread from high to low control is made even finer by different levels of control built into all the techniques employed to collect data. Observations, questionnaires, interviews, experiments, documentary, historical and comparative studies can each be structured, semi-structured or unstructured, giving a wide choice from naturalistic to fully experimental.

It is this control and its specification that distinguishes social research from journalism. But it does not only consist of constraints over the researcher and the researched to ensure that reliability and validity can be assessed. There is also control imposed by the overt or covert influence of the theories, models or networks of the researchers. The direction of control over the way data are collected and more importantly the way that data are analysed will depend on the theoretical position adopted in the design of the work and on the percolation of such influences into the interpretation of results. That is illustrated in Controversies 3, 4, 6, 7 and 9. This contamination joins the political and related bias that can appear in journalism and social research. It is why there was a fourth key question in the Introduction. The researcher should spell out the theoretical position adopted to enable the reader to ask questions about reliability and validity. The reader should look for this and for any intrusion of theory not spelled out. That applies in naturalistic as well as highly controlled work.

WHAT REALLY WENT ON UNDER THE BANYAN TREES?

Controversy 1 detailed the nature-nurture debate which Margaret Mead was to affect decisively with her study of adolescent girls in Samoa.[1] The view of adolescence in the 1920s was dominated by Stanley Hall's studies around the turn of the century.[2] Hall was one of the new school of empiricist psychologists, observing the behaviour of young people, building up a model of universal, inevitable rebellion during development. That view rested on the then dominant evolutionary and biological theories that went back to Galton and Darwin. Not only was adolescence a period of storm and stress, but this was a recapitulation in each developing individual of the early stages in human evolution. Each lived through the primitive phases of human life. The alternative, psychoanalytical view of Freud that was published at the same time as Hall described adolescence as the period when the conflicts of infancy were resolved into reproductive, adult sex.[3] This was similarly influenced by the view that the primitive id lay beneath the surface of civilised behaviour. Individuals once again re-capitulated the stages of increasing civilisation as they matured. Both theories of adolescence had a biological, evolutionary base and saw it as a time of inevitable stress or anxiety as the savage was controlled while the child matured into civilised, normal adulthood.

Into this academic climate of biological determinism stepped young Margaret Mead. She was an American, the daughter of agnostic middle-class parents, born in Philadelphia in 1901 and a doctoral student of Franz Boas.[4] In 1928 she published *Coming of Age in Samoa*. It proved to be the best-selling of all anthropological books exerting influence at two levels. First, it countered the biological determinism that gave the dominant influence on human behaviour to inherited factors. The untroubled adolescent Samoan experience was so unlike that in western societies that biology couldn't be determining all human development. Neither could humanity be reproducing a primitive stage of development. So influential was the book that it was used to press the case for cultural determinism, thus replacing one way of seeing humans in the grip of forces beyond their control by another. At the second level the book exploded the current view that adolescence was a time of inevitable storm and stress. The account of the relaxed sexual and social life of Samoan girls suggested that any stress was created by social conditions, and hence remediable, rather than the unfolding of universal biological make-up.

There is little gain in this substitution of cultural for biological determinism. Sociologists came to see adolescence as the period when children were socialised into adult roles. The individual was seen as moulded by social expectations until adult status was achieved. Hall saw adolescents moving to civilised adult normality. Freud saw them as moving to normal adult reproductive sex and Parsons, the most prominent functionalist sociologist of the 1960s, saw them as being socialised into normality within the social system.[5] In none of these cases was there much room for individuality or for the adolescent to influence his or her own future.

The question that Mead set out to answer was 'Were the difficulties due to being adolescent or to being adolescent in America'.[6] The current psychological view in the 1920s was that 'rebellion against authority, philosophical perplexities, the flowering of idealism, conflict and struggle' should be ascribed to physical development. Yet as an anthropologist she saw attitudes as dependent upon social environment. The answer to her question 'Can we think of adolescence as a time in the life history of every girl child which carries with it symptoms of conflict and stress as surely as it implies a change in the girls body' was a firm 'No'.

Mead was twenty-three when she arrived in Samoa in 1925. She stayed for nine months, mainly in a government school whose female students were the respondents used in the study of adolescence. In her biography she confesses to knowing little about methods, to knowing what to look for but not how and of feeling despair at the situation. There is a cautious Appendix on methods in the book. The limitations of the interviews, the description of the social structure of the nearby villages, a questionnaire and of the psychological tests used in Samoa are listed. But Freeman has collected together evidence to show that her account of Samoan life was 'fundamentally in error'.[7] This was partly because of her inadequate knowledge of the language. It was partly her dependence on respondents who may have been teasing or deceiving her. Above all it was through slack control over her own search for evidence that would confirm her view that adolescent turmoil was missing and that sexual relations were casual. To Freeman, Mead was guilty of exampling, gathering up data to support her thesis and ignoring that which did not fit.

The objection of Samoans to Mead's work was the starting point for Freeman's investigation. *Coming of Age* is an affectionate account of Samoa, but for a people who prized virginity in females it must have seemed odd that Mead found so many of her respondents remembering casual lovemaking under the palms. So must the picture of Samoans as a gentle, uncompetitive people. Having seen Samoans playing rugby football against Tongans it is difficult to accept Mead's picture, just as it is difficult to accept that a small-scale society could be organised to accept unfettered sexual relations among adolescents.

The most telling criticism of Mead's work is that she may have accepted evidence from secondary and suspect sources. Central to her view that free lovemaking was expected among adolescents is her explanation of how this is reconcilable with the presentation of proof of female virginity at marriage. This proof is demanded by the 'talking chief', the spokesman of the bridegroom. Mead leaves this unexplained in *Coming of Age in Samoa*. But later, she solves the problem by stating that where the bride is not a virgin, chicken's blood is substituted. Freeman reports that Samoan chiefs were outraged by this account. Mead obtained this information, not from Samoans, but from one Phoebe Parkinson, who, when she gave it, had not been in Samoa since 1881, some fifty years earlier, having only then spent two weeks in a Samoan village. She had never been where Mead did her fieldwork. Furthermore, Freeman maintains that Mead elaborated this account in later books. Certainly in her autobiography, *Blackberry Winter* (1972), she seems to confirm the hearsay nature of the evidence that the bride who was discovered to have lost her virginity before marriage was punished, not for her promiscuity, but for not bringing an adequate supply of chicken blood to the ceremony.[8] As Freeman states, this completely misrepresents 'the attitude of the dignified and punctilious Samoans toward one of their most sancrosanct traditional institutions'.

It would be wrong to accept Freeman's criticisms without question. He has been criticised in the South Pacific for painting too violent a picture of Samoa. Furthermore, Mead's account of Samoa remains a remarkable achievement given the prevailing views of adolescence in the 1920s. There are accounts of Samoa that suggest that young people there face similar problems and opportunities for sexual experiment as their peers in the rest of the world.[9] Above all Mead made the general public aware of the variety of ways in which societies were organised and in which behaviour is manifested. She may have been careless of facts, indifferent about details, but she made a lasting contribution to bringing justice into the lives of women. Biological determinism had provided a reason for avoiding action to ensure equal opportunities for women. Mead used her work and her influence in good causes. But however influential, it has been challenged as unreliable.

There is an irony in this charge of unreliability in Mead's fieldwork.[10] She wrote at least three major works on anthropological methods. In one of these she details the care that needs to be taken to obtain a sample of respondents that represent the complete cultural experience. Yet in the search for a crucial piece of evidence to complete her case she was apparently willing to rely on hearsay from someone who was neither in the sample nor even involved in the culture studied.

There is little doubt that adolescence is a time of rapid, often radical, physical and social change. Biology and culture play a part. In retrospect, however, the evidence of Hall, Freud and of sociologists such as Parsons is too certain, implying universality and uniformity, where the anthropological evidence, however flawed, suggests variety and resilience. Many contemporary views of adolescence have not moved far from storm and stress. Instead of this being caused biologically it is seen as the product of expectations by both parents and the young themselves.[11] The images behind these expectations are pressed in the mass media. The image of the sloppy, rebellious adolescents of the 1980s isn't far from Hall's storm-tossed or Freud's sexually-anxious youth at the turn of the century. What has changed is the perceived role of the adolescents. At the start of the century they were passive, seen by social scientists as swept along by biology, physiology, sexuality. Now they are given an active role as culture users, adjusting their behaviour according to their image of themselves.[12] At least they have been accorded their humanity. This view also removes any inevitable period of stress. Some may go through adolescence serenely. Others do not. Mead's contribution confirms this at the level of societies. Social anthropology is an antidote to a Eurocentric view of the world.

3

INTERPRETIVE SOCIAL SCIENCE

We now go out of the laboratory, away from surveys designed in offices and from questionnaires and interviews derived from preconceived models, and into the field to observe, listen and interpret. Here you let the data come to you and formulate theories as you make sense of them. We are in the world of observation, of ethnography where the aim is to understand the world of drug addicts, tramps, jazz musicians, street gangs and fascists as well as pupils, students, workers and the unemployed. Instead of assuming that they know and can theorise about human behaviour and organisation in advance, interpretive social scientists go into the field to learn about others and, as they do so, about themselves.

However, preconceptions based in the theories and evidence of sociology or some other social science will still guide observation and interpretation. Indeed, this discipline distinguishes ethnography from journalism and other attempts to make sense of a new situation, a strange group or a foreign country in everyday life. All are trying to understand what is going on from the viewpoint of those observed. It will be confusing and very likely misinterpreted. Social scientists are distinguished only by the theories and methods that control their observations. But no academic detachment can now cushion the contact with those investigated.

There are a range of approaches available. Participant observation allows researchers to observe with minimum or nil disturbance from their presence. At the other extreme the researcher can use observation schedules and tests. A mix of methods is common. It enables results from each technique to be triangulated, cross-checked, and often gives the security of quantitative data. McGagny and Skipper don't just observe their strippers on the backstage;[1] they measure their vital statistics to compare with more or less endowed females. The researchers are marked out from journalists and others by using methods of observing, recording and theorising that are systematic and which are made public in accounts of the work. From Malinowski's *Argonauts of the Western Pacific* published in 1922,[2] there have been conventional ways of collecting data on particular types of event. Ethnography is a discipline and the methods used and the control exercised are still supposed to be made public.

This emphasis on the relevance of questions of reliability, validity and the publications of methods in interpretive research puts it into the scientistic category. The real alternative to this is to reject objectivity as a goal or even as a possibility and to adopt a political stance that the investigation of human affairs should not be detached but involved, aimed to improve the lot of those studied. The concern is not to put humanity under the telescope or microscope, but to act to remove injustice. The underlying questions are now about the morality of treating humans as objects for study, particularly when research is usually focussed on the poor and the penalised. Interpretive research as much as quantitative is seen as part of the apparatus of repression because it is detached and top-down.

The interpretive approach to research

There are many labels for research aimed to uncover the way people try to understand their situations. Field, qualitative, ethogenic ethnographic, anthropological, interpretive, naturalistic, phenomeno-logical, observational, grounded, case study, portrayal, illuminative and holistic are a few in use. Sometimes it is simply labelled an account. Halfpenny found social scientists at an S.S.R.C. symposium in 1978 also using terms such as soft, flexible, descriptive, subjective, illustrative and relativistic to describe this approach.[3] There are books on strategies. There are collections of accounts of actual research activity. The most striking feature of the method is flexibility. In interpretive research you have to be quick on your feet, not bound into a fixed programme of work often sub-contracted out to interviewers. There has also to be sensitivity towards the individuals observed, or there is a risk of imposing concepts and questions, categories, theories on them and on their situation.

Burgess identifies four common features of interpretive research.[4] First, the researcher tries not to disturb the natural setting. Second, the research design can be altered to allow for unexpected yet important findings as they turn up. Third, the focus is on social processes and the meanings given to them by participants. Fourth, data collection and analysis occur together. The contrast with traditional scientific method comes from the effort not to disturb the natural situation and to be alert to the interpretations of those being studied. There can be no preconceived and immutable research design because the researcher does not assume that he knows the way the situation is structured in advance of the enquiry. The accounts by interpretive researchers show how nimble they had to be to follow up unexpected leads. The search is for validity. Reliability takes second place.

Efforts to preserve the natural setting usually involve some form of participation to minimise disturbance. Among researchers investigating schools, Hargreaves,[5] Lacey,[6] Ball,[7] and Burgess[8] taught to help in being accepted. Despite being kicked in the teeth by researchers while giving away free cups of coffee and plenty of time, teachers and others are usually hospitable. Where such a welcome for researchers is unlikely, covert methods have been used. In Britain these include studies of the National Front (Fielding),[9]* Pentacostal groups (Homan),[10] and Scientologists (Wallis).[11] Humphreys lurking around men's lavatories is an American example.[12]

The value of getting into the natural situation can be seen in studies of the hidden economy. Economic models of the market, of money supply, or an investment-driven system ignore pilfering, tax fiddling, moonlighting, fixing overtime and fringe benefits. Sociologists working within this black economy have shown how normal working relationships can incorporate petty crime. Within private and public sectors of the economy work is made rewarding by individual enterprise, albeit dishonestly.

* Since the publication of the third edition, Dr Fielding has pointed out that as his interviews with officials of the National Front were overt, his research cannot be accurately described as covert. The Publishers are happy to take the opportunity of a reprint to make this clear.

These studies have to be clandestine. Ditton becomes a bread roundsman.[13] Henry becomes a driver, cellarman and sales assistant for a wines and spirits merchant.[14] Mars makes himself at home in the docks.[15] This is a long way from a survey organised in an office, or a controlled experiment. Ethnography is open-ended, organised to maximise the chances of the unexpected being observed. It can be fun, it can be dangerous, but it's always unpredictable. Inside the human lot it makes sense to those involved, but can confuse researchers until they learn the score. Fletcher has provided one researcher's despairing account of feeling overwhelmed by the wealth of data.[16] Yet the alternative is to assume that you understand, model the situation and survey it. The feeling of ignorance when first in the field as an ethnographer is a warning against scientistic methods that assume you don't need to be there to find out and understand before applying questionnaires or interviewing.

The flexibility during research does not only include acting fast if furtively to preserve the natural situation when the disguise starts to slip. Many researchers have reported rapid shifts to follow up new clues and promising leads. Switching the design of an experiment or survey would break the link to the model behind the methods and destroy the logic in the methodology. In interpretive research barriers can be by-passed and side-turnings investigated because it is searching for hypotheses not testing them. In some cases changes of direction have been necessary because the original design was faulty. Hammersley starts observing and recording in the class-rooms of a secondary modern school, but pays increasing attention to chat overheard in the staffroom.[17] Jenkins reports that in the evaluation of the Schools Cultural Studies Project in Northern Ireland, 'secondary agendas' were encouraged.[18] In his study of Scientology, Wallis, unexpectedly given a mailing list of members, designs and dispatches a postal questionnaire.[19] Only later, having interviewed backsliders, sent the questionnaire and attended a scientology course did he inform the organisation that he was researching them. It is no surprise that the published account was received with little enthusiasm by those studied.[20]

Most interpretive studies of schools have concentrated on the definitions established by teachers and pupils as they interact. King has shown how pupils and teachers come to share meanings in infant schools.[21] Woods has described *Teacher Strategies*[22] and *Pupil Strategies*[23] as well as the way these are reconciled in secondary schools. Most of these studies paint a picture of meanings being adjusted by both parties in the classroom. Teachers do it to survive or to retain control. Pupils do it to relieve boredom or make life bearable. Pupils and teachers give meaning to the situation in the classroom. We are in the world of interactions and processes not attainments and outcomes.

The most striking contrast between conventional scientistic and interpretive research is in the role of theory. The former is designed to test. In the latter, theories, hypotheses, categories and concepts are developed as data is collected and analysed. Theory is supposed to emerge from the data. It is grounded. This use of grounded theory, recommended by Glaser and Strauss is a particular attraction of interpretive research.[24] It relieves the researcher of having to work from theory to design. This operationalisation is difficult. Working out theories as you go along sounds easier. In practice it is not. The emerging theory may not suggest what data to collect next. Thus, Porter found that she could not decide what were the theoretically important data to start with.[25]

A detailed account of the way theory develops with the research is given by Turner.[26] He reviews available models of interaction in the school, decides to focus on the way pupils deal with particular situations, and on perspectives from their viewpoint. Hence data are collected by informal conversation, unstructured interview and observation. The design is an attempt to eliminate the pre-conceptions of the researcher. As Turner collects data the varied responses of pupils become apparent. These change over time and in different contexts. Pro and anti-school groups are not always conformist or deviant. The motivations for being pro or anti vary widely. Here theory is grounded in the data and progressively elaborated. But it was there at the start. That is a key point, central to the discussion in Chapter 1. Even where the methods used require no pre-conceived imposition of categories of behaviour and motivation, there is some theory present. With Turner it is explicit and rightly discussed in full. If it was implicit, which is the more common case, the reader is left to guess how it creeps into the interpretation of the data when they are analysed.

What weight can be put on observational studies?

It must have struck many teachers that accounts of their classrooms by ethnographers sitting in for a few sessions, unused to the school, not knowing the children or the curriculum, the school organisation or events preceding the research are arrogant in their assumption that the account produced reflects reality. Why is this outsider able to produce a more valid and reliable account than the teacher who has an extended and intimate knowledge of the class? It certainly is not because of inexperience in observation, for that is at the heart of teaching as it is of ethnography. The parallel is with an H.M.I. inspection. How do these outsiders, popping in for a few hours report with such authority?

This question was taken up by McNamara in 1980.[27] He describes three aspects of the 'Outsider's arrogance'. These were:
1. The data presented are suspect, full of interpretations by the researcher that can be challenged.
2. The researcher's inferences about the meanings attributed to events by teachers or pupils are presented as unproblematical.
3. The researcher's interpretations often call on complex theories to explain events rather than often simpler explanations connected with the everyday workings of classrooms.

McNamara was vigorously counter-attacked by Hammersley, one of those criticised.[28] He points out that McNamara presented no basis for the superiority of his alternative explanations. That is, however, merely to confirm that there is no way of confirming one view against another. In reality there is no easy way of establishing the credence of accounts. Insider and outsider interpretations are different, but all are real to those holding them. That is however of little comfort to the reader who usually has little information from which to judge how much weight to put upon each.

The ORACLE (Observational Research and Classroom Learning Evaluation) project was based at the University of Leicester from 1975. This large-scale, longitudinal study in three L.E.A.s, focused on the top primary age group, was concerned mainly with the effectiveness of different teaching approaches across the primary school curriculum. Later the study extended into transfer to secondary schooling. A summary of the methods used is available in Galton and Delamont.[29]

The observational data in primary schools were collected through two standardised instruments, a teacher and a pupil record. These were carefully planned schedules attempting to maximise reliability among the observers. There was also participant observation to follow up children in the classrooms. It was this ethnographic part of the work that has been a major concern to the team. The observers were in different schools, in different towns. There was no attempt to standardise the way field notes were to be taken and no training of the observers. The latter is acknowledged as a major weakness and Galton and Delamont give examples of very different records of the same events from experienced and novice observers.

The reliability of observations is easier to check in a large project such as ORACLE with several observers in a large team. Most ethnography is done by lone researchers where cross-checking is impossible. It is rare for there to be retrospective examination as in Controversy 3. The recommended technique to improve reliability is triangulation. In practice this boils down to using different strategies in research so they can be cross-checked. Denzin recommends triangulation, multiple approaches, at the levels of theories, methods, data and investigators.[30] In the ORACLE project explicit theory is not considered. There were different methods and many investigators, but Galton and Delamont very honestly report that triangulation was never even considered during the project. Reconciling the participant observation data with the teacher and pupil records, the test scores and questionnaires did prove difficult. The ORACLE team adopted the usual procedure of accepting the quantitative data as 'fact', with observational data as illumination.

There remains the problem of observer reliability and validity. The normal one-person observational study is difficult to assess. The reader has to rely on the credibility of the account given, however scant. The political views and theoretical position of the researcher have often to be guessed at.

Part of the problem can be overcome in team research by training observers. In the ORACLE project this was done to improve reliability in the use of the teacher and the pupil record. Observers undertook a paid two-week course using video and practising in classrooms. They were only employed if they reached a satisfactory standard when their observations were compared with those of experienced users of the Records. Training is easy when there is a standard observational instrument to be used. But ethnography depends on observing the natural situation. The researcher is alert for the unpredicted and the theoretically interesting. Here flexibility and an acute eye for the significant is at a premium. Yet that is just the perception most likely to be affected by the preconceived views of researchers. The question about reliability is tough for ethnography. Validity is also to be queried because what is seen will be guided by preconceptions.

The observational studies that have involved teams have often run into problems as interpretations of events clash. In Britain an example is the acrimonious account by Bell of the research during the second Banbury study directed by Stacey in the early 1970s.[31] The organisation of the work was seen as not sufficiently clear to define where authority lay, leading to disputes between Stacey the director of the project, and Bell in charge of its execution. Such conflicts are most common when alternative interpretations of data have to be reconciled or published alongside each other.

In the account of the Keele Integrated Studies Project there are chapters and inserted comments from participants in the project and from teachers. These show that my interpretation of events was often seen as wrong by those being observed.[32] These critical views had to be accepted because the evaluation was designed to show the different definitions of the curriculum project among those involved. These different views were published because they were so contrasting that publication could only be achieved by offering those in dispute a chance to air their interpretations in print. Behind interpretive research is the theory that reality is what people define as real. Ethnographers search for meanings because they account for why people behave in individual ways. Attempts to smooth out contrasts in published accounts can be misleading. The publication of Bell's account of the Banbury restudy was accompanied by so much hassle that Bell's co-researchers would not waive their rights under the British libel laws. They saw Bell's account as personal, leaving out his own shortcomings and ignoring the most profound problem in sociological work of the tension between completing the job in hand and maintaining a commitment to the subject.[33]

The limits of observation

The difficulties in assessing the credibility of ethnographic accounts arises partly from the difficulties in seeing what was actually done from the very limited amount of information usually provided for the reader. But even where sufficient description is given on the methods used, the ambitions in the exercise remain a reason for caution. The observer is attempting to get into the mind of those observed to uncover how they are making sense of the situation. Yet the common-sense frameworks for interpreting events may bear little relation to the theoretical frameworks brought to bear by the researcher. Glue sniffers may feel alienated from post-industrial urban society and unemployed youth may reject the work ethics of capitalism, but these are not the language of those usually observed. Ethnography acknowledges the existence of these two levels of interpretation and is consequently an advance on top-down scientistic research. But it can still contain imposed interpretations of the researchers.

The most suspect accounts are those where the reader is presented with an interpretation as if the researchers had some 'hey presto' access to the mind of those studied, but with no details on why this is to be believed. For example, Marsh, Rosser and Harré, in their book *The Rules of Disorder*,[34] produce a study 'Trouble in School' that looks at the way pupils and teachers interact. Here however there is no prevarication. The school is seen as the type that has not adapted itself to alternative, non-academic needs and which, in general, is not sensitive to the fact that pupils are people with as much right as anyone else to be respected. The pupils were seen to be seeking to establish their power within the classrooms to counterbalance perceived affronts to their dignity. Now this may be true and unquestionably does happen. But there is no way of telling from the information provided in this account. Indeed, while the insensitivity of the teachers is reported as half the problem, there are no accounts of the teachers' views as there are of the pupils. There is also no indication of checks being made on the accounts given by these pupils. If they felt devalued by the teachers and that their dignity was being affronted, how did they feel about these academics being around the school? Some of the accounts suggest some rather curious questions from the researchers, but these are not included. The reader is left to guess how the passages included were selected. There is not even any detail on the number of visits to the school, on its organisation and environment nor of the relations with the staff.

This study, as with most of these classroom investigations, covers relations between teachers and pupils, but does not include anything from the former. The difficulty may be partly teacher reluctance to contribute. It is partly that the interest is in the underdog view. But the omission is, particularly in the light of the theoretical position taken, reprehensible. It is similar to the failure to include accounts from the police alongside those of delinquents when discussing labelling. But this omission is part of a wider neglect of the issue of reliability. It is possible to collect accounts from participants in different positions and check them to see if there are discrepancies. It is possible to check accounts from the same person at different times. There are great difficulties in interpreting audio and video tapes. It is the unspoken and not only the words that give the message. Responses are influenced by the researcher and the subject of the research. Some check is necessary and those checks need to be reported to the reader. If they are not, scepticism is appropriate. Researchers are guilty of unreliability until proved innocent.

The final question for interpretive research is whether it can ever reflect the complex reality of classrooms, schools and other groupings. Barrow criticising the ORACLE project cannot see even this large-scale project getting near to uncovering the reasons why the 489 children studied progressed at different rates.[35] There is information on categories of teaching, on pupil learning styles and on some relations between them. But in each situation there will be hundreds of factors at work for each child to produce optimal learning conditions and few of the possibilities will have been touched on in the research. Barrow likens the attempt to research learning in classrooms to trying to conceptualise, operationalise and measure 'love'. Interpretive research does less violence to reality than survey or experiment. But the reliability and validity of work on love and spring is likely to be low. It should always be questioned.

PART *2*

TECHNIQUES FOR COLLECTING INFORMATION

Social research consists of data collection sandwiched between two layers of creativity. The first layer has been described in Part 1. Through the use of metaphors and models the world is structured for the researcher so that it can be investigated in line with other enquiries organised within a scientific community. Whether the aim is to test hypotheses or to find them, to find the case that refutes or the examples that confirm, the theorising that precedes the data collection is creative. Once the data are gathered in, their analysis and interpretation are again creative. Whether the data are referred back to the model that guided the work or to produce new explanations, this is a time for imagination. This is the subject of Part 3.

It is this view of research that accounts for this section on techniques being squeezed into the middle of the book. Most manuals on how to do research start with techniques. But the strengths as well as the limitations stem from the 'logy' part of methodology. That is how data are given their meaning and related to existing knowledge. That is why it is essential for researchers, including students writing essays as well as the Office of Population Censuses and Surveys, to spell out the reasons why techniques were adopted, analyses made and conclusions drawn. The same criteria apply in all cases where evidence is being presented. The four questions in the Introduction apply in this part in particular. But this involves spelling out the rationale of the research and that necessitates reference back to the models that reduce the complexity of the social world to a scale that could be investigated, albeit selectively.

HAS COMPREHENSIVE SCHOOLING RAISED OR LOWERED STANDARDS IN EDUCATION?

Controversy 2 discussed the difficulties in detecting whether schools make any impact on pupil progress once the school context is taken into account. Given this problem in detecting school effects, it is unlikely that the differences in the standards achieved by a selective or a comprehensive secondary school system could be detected. Yet it is an important question, generates a lot of political heat and provides a dispute that illustrates the way research designs are riddled with implicit or explicit political assumptions.

In 1977 the D.E.S. funded the National Children's Bureau (N.C.B.) to use its National Child Development Survey data to compare the progress of the 7,866 children in comprehensive and in secondary modern and grammar schools.[1] This is an important case of *ex post facto* experimentation.

Progress in Secondary Schools, published in 1980, reported scores on reading comprehension and mathematics of the children when aged 11 and 16 years. There were few differences in progress between (non-selective) comprehensive schools on one side and grammar and secondary modern schools (selective) on the other. In particular, those at the top end of ability were doing as well in comprehensive as in grammar schools.

Press response was predictable. The *Daily Express* headline was 'Full marks: comprehensive schools come out on top of the class for bright youngsters'.[2] The *Times Educational Supplement* reported 'Brightest do as well in all-in schools'.[3] The fun started two months later in September when Cox and Marks, both doughty campaigners on the political Right and Black Paper contributors, published a lengthy critique entitled *Real Concern*.[4] This attacked technical weaknesses and suggested that the data were doctored. In October the N.C.B. counter-attacked with *Real Research*.[5] In December both parties, Steedman, Fogelman and Hutchinson from the N.C.B. and Cox and Marks met for a symposium at the University of Exeter. Predictably this meeting only confirmed the disagreement, the N.C.B. contingent even objecting to Cox and Marks contributing to this academic get-together.[6]

Cox and Marks focused on the reading test used by the N.C.B. researchers at age 11 and 16. This is a wide age spread and by 16 the more able children would be likely to be bunched at the top. Just where discrimination was needed, there was a ceiling compressing the scores. The remaining major criticisms were about access to the data and to the partiality of the N.C.B. researchers, and even to influence upon them by unspecified but vested interests. The remarkable aspect of this dispute is not the technical criticisms. Many appear in the report of the symposium (see for example papers by King, Preece, Evans and Wrigley in Dancy, 1981).[7] Its main feature was the bitterness between the parties. In April 1981, the British Educational Research Association criticised Cox and Marks for using language that went beyond that normally acceptable.[8] But a lot was at stake as comprehensive schools spread, and the accusations that political bias had worked through to the N.C.B. evidence was to remain on the agenda when the next episode in trying to compare comprehensive and selective schooling emerged in 1983. In this case, the centre of attention was *Standards in English Schools* by Marks, Cox and Pomian-Srzednicki, concluding that '... the calculations show, consistently and robustly, that substantially higher O-level, CSE and A-level examination results are to be expected for pupils in a fully selective system than a fully comprehensive system'.[9] The critical response was expectedly fast and furious.

The *Times Educational Supplement* was first with a comment under the editorial headline 'Where research and advocacy meet', claiming that Marks and Cox discovered what they set out to find.[10] Marks and Cox were in print next week objecting to this 'inaccurate and partial' editorial (*TES*, 8.7.83).[11] Even more remarkable was an instantaneous and detailed technical review by Gray, already the scourge of earlier major studies by Bennett (1976) and Rutter (1979) in the same issue of the *TES*.[12] Gray's criticisms were based on his own research and focused on the weak control over social class exerted by Marks, Cox and Pomian-Szrednicki. Second, Gray pointed to the creamed structure of many comprehensive schools that made comparisons hazardous. The following week, Gray and Jones published yet another critique of *Standards in English Schools*, presenting a re-analysis of the examination results used by the Marks and Cox team.[13] Gray and Jones found the results anything but robust. Building in a stronger measure of social background they report that up to 80 per cent of differences in examination results were explained by differences in the social and intellectual composition of the intakes into schools. The selective or non-selective nature of the schools seemed barely relevant. We were back with the evidence on school effects. They diminish once the social background of the children is taken into account.

The following weeks of correspondence in the *TES* were hilarious. Professor Flew, another Black Paper contributor, attacked Gray's critiques but with some obscure references to other works.[14] Gray responded with two cheques for £50, one for Flew's favourite charity if he could verify the existence of a review referred to in his letter, the other £50 was for Flew himself if he could produce a review by Professor Wrigley also mentioned.[15] Professor Wrigley, seeming bemused, wrote to the *TES* on 19.8.83 to say with some justice that he found these disputes over standards unenlightening and unhelpful, but not whether he had received the cheque.[16] But not even that wisdom could stop the tide of battle.

The next development was unexpected. Rumours appeared in the press that the D.E.S. was to fund further work by Cox and Marks.[17] By December 1983 there were leaks of exchanges between them and the D.E.S. statisticians following comments on *Standards in English Schools*. Sir Keith Joseph reassured Parliament that the D.E.S. did not consider *Standards in English Schools* seriously flawed.[18] The problem arose after the publication by D.E.S. of Statistical Bulletin 16/83.[19] These bulletins do not usually stir the blood, but in this case the D.E.S. statisticians confirmed Gray's claim that the overwhelming factor behind examination results is the social composition of the area around a school.

Inevitably this must have annoyed Cox and Marks as it must have delighted Gray. Significantly it also confirms a long tradition of educational research relating school and social class.

This is a dismal chapter in recent research history. Marks, Cox

and Pomian-Srzednicki continue to analyse examination res
and in 1986 laid into the I.L.E.A., thus stirring up a similar dispute
to that in 1983.[20] The articles and letters to the *TES* in April, May
and June 1986 largely featuring Cox and Marks in one corner and
Stubbs and Mortimore from the I.L.E.A. in the other are a re-run
of the earlier technical and political arguments.[21] These seem to be
inseparable because of the difficulties in designing this analysis of
examination results. Different designs produce very different
results and, not surprisingly, researchers seem to choose designs
that lead to the results that they expect.

ING

Research is always based on samples whether carefully selected for a survey or hastily picked as an illustration for an argument. Furthermore, such samples are frequently the basis for generalisation about the population from which they have been drawn. Sampling is a systematic way of choosing a group small enough to study and large enough to be representative. The importance of scrutinising samples has increased with the popularity of interpretive research, particularly as it is usually very difficult to detect how and why the particular case was chosen.

Sampling illustrates a recurring theme throughout the technical part of this book. Research implies method in investigation, not the slap-happy collection of information. The key to this is control, exercised over the means of collection and over the researcher. Thus sampling is a means of control. Researchers arrange for the sample to be picked for them not by them. The means of selection are the subjects of this chapter.

There has been much generalisation from inadequate samples. The case for and against comprehensive schooling or mixed ability grouping have been backed by examples intentionally selected to slant the evidence. That is appropriate for politicians or inspectors who prescribe. It is not the way to dependable description. However, researchers often lose control of their evidence as it is used to support a case. Thomas was typical in looking back to his work on *The Polish Peasant* across twenty years and confessing an aversion to it because of the way others had used it without reference to his methodological cautions.[1]

It may be difficult to define a population to be studied. Old people or adolescents are not contained in single lists and arbitrary selection has to be made from incomplete sources such as cooperative general practitioners. Criminals are sampled from prison or court records. But in these and other cases there is no exact definition of the population from which a sample can be drawn. If you do not know in advance who are included as 'men in the street', it is questionable whether you can ever sample them in a representative way.

At worst a writer's views may be serving as a one-man sample. In other cases convenience or availability may have determined the sample. Unless the method of sampling is spelled out, scepticism is advisable. Students from one university department of psychology are unlikely to represent all students, all young persons or the human race. Monkeys caged in a zoo are unlikely to provide pertinent evidence for the explanation of normal human behaviour. Asylums, concentration camps and factories are often used to generalise about the organisation of schools, but it is worth remembering the differences between model and reality. However reliable the methods used in sampling, the group selected may only be representative of the specific population from which it was chosen.

This need to consider the representativeness of samples applies in all subjects. The historian has to be wary of generalising about a past population from evidence left by the rich who could afford to build to last and could leave written records. Anthropologists often observed the unusual rather than the normal and by the time observational techniques had improved, most of the small-scale societies had been colonised or fought over in the Second World War. The criminologist relied on criminals who had been caught rather than those successful in getting away with crime. In all subjects the most certain way of ensuring that a work is published is to concentrate on the problems and the deviations. This is legitimate provided these are not taken as a sample of the whole population.

There are two forms of sample used in the social sciences. The judgement, purposive or quota samples are all variations on the method of selecting individuals or groups who are seen to be representative of the target population. The judgement is that of the researcher, choosing what seems to him typical, relevant or interesting. It is purposive because the choice serves the objectives of the investigation. The quota sample allows the actual collector of information to use discretion in the final choice. The probability sample by contrast is selected as far as possible to eliminate the judgement or bias of the investigator. These are sometimes called random samples because at its most refined each member of the population is given an equal chance of selection. However, lucky dips are seldom used. It is more common to take a systematic sample from a list of names. Electoral registers, doctors' lists and record cards can be used to draw every *n*th name according to the total size of sample required.

Random samples do not guarantee representativeness. It is bad, but random luck, to draw a sample of all millionaires in a study of income distribution. It is small consolation that from a random sample the chances of this producing the results found can be calculated. Large samples reduce this kind of mischance, but are expensive. Only the Census draws a 100 per cent or a 10 per cent sample of the whole population.

The more usual procedure to ensure representation without excessive size is through stratification. This consists of breaking the population down into smaller homogeneous groups before sampling. A box of a hundred marbles, ten of ten different colours, could be sampled adequately by choosing one from each of the ten colours after they had been separated. To sample them and ensure representation without this stratification would take a much larger sample than ten. Stratification reduces the chance of fluke samples and enables the proportions in each strata to be fixed in advance. Hence most random samples ensure not an even chance of selection, but a known chance.

Judgement and probability samples are often combined. Thus a school or a factory may be selected first because it is convenient for the researcher. Then a random sample is taken within. For the reader this combination is important. The initial choice may have introduced bias which can be concealed under the mathematical calculations based on the second, random sampling. The examples that follow have been chosen because the methods of sampling are discussed by the author. The most suspicious are those where there is no information on the sampling.

Probability sampling

The term probability sampling is used because random selection enables the possibility of results occurring by chance to be calculated. That is the meaning of significance levels. One per cent significance means that there is a one in a hundred chance that the results were due to the sample chosen. It is the security of this calculation that leads government in particular to use probability sampling. Furthermore, governments can usually obtain high response in their surveys. If this cannot be obtained a purposive sample that avoids response problems is often preferable.

The D.E.S. Assessment of Performance Unit (A.P.U.) regularly monitors educational standards in language, mathematics and science. Most discussion on the A.P.U.'s Statistics Advisory Group was over the size of sample required to get reliable results.[2] It needed to be large enough to give sufficient numbers for sub-groups, such as boys and girls, in schools of different sizes, types and in different regions of the country. Even a very large sample can produce very small numbers once such sub-divisions are made. But large samples are expensive and are a burden to schools. This could raise non-response. The sample size for A.P.U. surveys was agreed at 10,000, chosen so that only small groups of children were affected at any one time in a school. At each survey a selected child only answers a small part of each test.

Each A.P.U. survey is based on a two-stage sample. The first stage is a random selection of schools, stratified by size, type and region. Then pupils are selected within each school according to their date of birth, with roughly equal numbers in each sampled school. In 1986, the age 15 science survey was based on 12,000 children from 483 schools and the age 13 survey on 15,000 children in 621 schools.[3] Headteachers withdrew 35 and 33 children respectively. Another 423 and 341 pupils were absent during the testing. But 106 schools were unable or unwilling to take part at 15 and 131 schools at age 13.

Her Majesty's Inspectors (H.M.I.) have surveyed each age phase of schooling in the last decade. The 1978 Primary Survey[4] and the 1979 Secondary Survey[5] were each based on samples randomly selected for H.M.I. However, the two middle school surveys, in 1983 and 1985, were selected by H.M.I. and only consisted of 48 schools for 9- to 13-year-olds[6] and 49 for the 8- to 12-year-olds.[7] It is honestly reported that these were not 'statistically representative samples', but results are still expressed with significance levels as if they were.

Purposive sampling

In probability sampling the individuals, groups and schools are picked by some formula from lists. In purposive sampling the researcher does the picking. A typical but very well documented case is in the study of Bishop McGregor School by Burgess (1984).[8] In 1972 Burgess found no ethnographic studies of comprehensive schools, the government had just announced that the leaving age was to be raised, and he was looking for a PhD topic. Burgess gets down to reading, meeting education officials and attends available meetings of teachers. At one meeting he is approached by a man who asks 'Who are you and where do you come from?' Not put off by the reply that he is speaking to a researcher at the University of Warwick, the stranger introduces himself as running Bishop McGregor Comprehensive School, gives Burgess his telephone number and asks him to visit if he would like to look round.

At the visit Burgess is clearly vetted by the headteacher, taken to lunch with staff, given access to some of the pupils and invited to come back to work. The sample school has fallen into his lap. Clearly there is no searching round for a pleasant school to work in, nor one that is likely to produce an account that will guarantee the sales of a book in this selection. But headteachers who volunteer their schools for investigation by sociologists certainly have confidence and probably little to hide. Above all, the judgement to accept was by Burgess. There is no claim to representativeness in the book and there is a candid and thorough account of the choice of school and the methods used.

Purposive sampling is common in the social sciences and in education. The reader should always question the reasons for the choice of institution studied. Why did the ORACLE project pick schools around the University of Leicester, where it was based?[9] Was there anything atypical about them? Does *Growing Up At The Margins* in the North-East differ from other regions?[10] Was

Hargreaves's Lumley Secondary Modern, the subject of the most influential school study of them all, representative of thousands of others outside the North-West?[11] Generalisations from psychology students at American universities, children at progressive schools for the well-off, criminals who have been caught and appear in court, headteachers who are keen for their school to be investigated can be very misleading bases for describing the human condition. Even more so are assorted samples of rats and monkeys cooped up in laboratories.

The term 'quota sampling' is often applied to the type of sampling used in market research and opinion polling. In quota sampling, the interviewer is given a list with the types of person to contact. These are usually defined by such criteria as social class, age and sex. The interviewer gets a list with the numbers she is to contact of each type. She goes, for example, to areas where the twelve working-class married women workers between twenty and thirty years old that make up one quota are liable to be found. Then there is a search for a specified number with these characteristics previously defined in the office. In practice quota sampling gives reliable results with experienced interviewers, but because it is not random, is not open to mathematical procedures that can give a level of confidence in the results obtained. The speed, cheapness and absence of problems of finding particular individuals make quota sampling useful, but it lacks the mathematical basis that can indicate the chances of the results from a random sample being due to the particular sample that has been used.

Quota sampling depends on the judgement of the investigator. The interviewer tempted to fill her quotas with the alert woman with one child rather than tackling a harried mother of four, although the latter really fits the quota definition, is in the same position as the research worker tempted to use school X instead of Y because the former is welcoming and convenient. In both personal bias is entering before information has been collected and the outcome may be tinged by this subjective element.

In some cases quota sampling has to be used because it is impossible to find lists from which a probability sample of population can be drawn. Thus there is no way of listing affluent workers or children of very high ability. They can only be sampled by choosing likely firms or schools and contacting those that fall within the definition of this particular population. The alternative is to take a very large probability sample and analyse separately those that fall into the appropriate categories.

One particularly hazardous form of purposive sampling is in the use of volunteers. Regardless of the safeguards that are built in, the reader is right to suspect that there is something ususual about those who step forward when a researcher asks for help. The most famous example of this kind is the Kinsey Report on human sexual behaviour.[12] Kinsey was determined to get a large sample and organised a campaign to interest clubs, families and other groups to volunteer. His object was to get 100 per cent samples from a number of different groups. However, while his final sample numbered 12,000, a minority were completed groups. Kinsey was aware of the dangers of volunteers and built in cross-checking techniques to detect distortions. This was a reason for wanting complete families or groups, for the answers could then be checked against others in the group.

The first volunteers were found to include many who were active, aggressive and exhibitionist. Kinsey tried therefore to obtain more reluctant volunteers by his recruiting campaign. He appealed for volunteers in the name of science, tried to establish advanced rapport in communities and to establish a reputation for scrupulous anonymity. But the suspicion remains that in such an intimate enquiry, those who come forward for interview are also those who are advanced in their behaviour. Furthermore, some groups such as homosexuals may be very reluctant to volunteer for fear of blackmail or prosecution, however secure the information was actually kept.

Dependence on volunteers is rare, but often someone in authority or position of influence may provide the volunteers. Work relying on such samples must be read as illustrations of the attitudes and behaviour of those who are cooperative or are not in a position to say no. Similarly, samples from those attending clubs, those at home during the day or using public libraries are not likely to be typical. A study such as Hemming's *Problems of Adolescent Girls*, based on 3,259 letters to a weekly journal between April 1953 and March 1955, is representative only of girls who write about their problems to magazine 'aunties'.[13] The greatest blunder in survey history was the 1936 Literary Digest poll, predicting that Landon would defeat Roosevelt, on the basis of a postal questionnaire from a sample drawn from the telephone directory, thus eliminating many poorer voters.[14]

There is no simple way of assessing whether a sample is adequate. Three important features of sampling have to be considered. First, as long as sampling is being used it is a matter of how much chance there is of freak samples being drawn, never a matter of certainty. This is why results from random sampling are expressed in terms of probability or levels of confidence. Second, the larger the sample, the more confidence there can be that a freak selection will not be made. Thirdly, the greater the variety of the characteristics in the population being measured the larger the sample needs to be. One tin soldier from thousands from the same run of production suffices as a test of quality. But the physical features of humans and even more their behaviour and attitudes are very varied and a larger sample is needed. The greater the spread of the feature being measured around the mean, the larger the sample size has to be. This is why stratification is commonly used, for it arranges the population into groups so that each contains persons of similar age, class, education and so on, thus reducing the necessary sample size. The confidence that can be placed in the adequacy of a sample therefore varies inversely with the distribution of the characteristics being measured and directly with the numbers in the sample.

Response

The care with which a sample has been designed will have been wasted if those chosen cannot be found or will not cooperate. Low response rate can ruin the reliability of a survey. The reader should search for evidence that response was considered as a design problem, that there were efforts to reduce non-response and that there was some attempt to investigate the characteristics of those who could not be found or slammed the door. The frankness of the author in discussing this issue is an indicator of a concern to give the reader a chance to assess the dependability of the work. The following are response rates in different types of survey.

Official committees

BULLOCK REPORT, *A Language for Life*, response rate 87.5 per cent.[15]

WARNOCK REPORT, *Special Educational Needs*, response rate for special schools and classes 56 per cent, for ordinary schools, 48 per cent.[16]

Office of Population Censuses and Surveys

GENERAL HOUSEHOLD SURVEY, response rate 72 per cent complete, 84 per cent partial, with 12 per cent of non-responders not wishing to take part and 2 per cent not contactable.[17]

Postal questionnaire

J. GABRIEL, *The Emotional Problems of the Teacher in the Classroom*, response rate to first questionnaire to teachers 35 per cent and to second questionnaire 29 per cent.[18]

F. MUSGROVE, *Youth and the Social Order*, response rate 32 per cent in towns, 34 per cent in suburbs.[19]

Survey using interviews

J. *and* E. NEWSON, *Infant Care in an Urban Community*, response rate 92 per cent, with 1.6 per cent refusals.[20]

Follow-up study

J. W. B. DOUGLAS, *The Home and the School*,[21] contained full information from 5,418 from sample first drawn in 1946. 4.3 per cent died and 4.5 per cent emigrated by 1950. This rose to 4.9 per cent and 6.7 per cent at the time of *The Home and the School* survey.

National survey

J. H. GOLDTHORPE, *Social Mobility and Class Structure in Modern Britain*,[22] response rate 81.8 per cent, with 4,440 of the original sample of 16,563 having died, being out of the age range of 20 to 64 specified, or moved from the address in the electoral register from which the sample was taken. 1,521 refused to cooperate, 12.1 of the total. The remainder of the non-respondents could not be contacted.

The low figure for response in such an important report as the Warnock Committee seems to have been due to sending the questionnaire to schools late in the summer term when most teachers were about to go on holiday. The Bullock committee surveyed in January. The figures show the very low response in postal questionnaires. Also, they show that very high responses are possible, if, as in the case of the Office of Population Censuses and Surveys, investment is made in following up those not contacted first time.

Returning to the A.P.U. we can now see the implication of possible non-representativeness, even with a sample of around 10,000. In early surveys, non-response rose from 4 per cent in 1978 to 11 per cent in 1980 for England. In science surveys it was 34 per cent in Northern Ireland for written tests by 1980. This non-response had increased overall to 30 per cent for 15-year-olds and for 13-year-olds in 1986. For England it was 21 and 23 per cent.[23] The likelihood was that the non-responders were among the lower attainers. This applies to schools as well as children. Absentees tend to be near the bottom of the form. Schools not responding are likely to be those with problems. With 10,000 children and nearly 500 schools the A.P.U. can still publish with some confidence. But two or three children from a sample of thirty when a class is sampled can raise average scores. In comparison, a school that conscientiously follows up the absentees and then tests them is likely to reduce its average score. A slack school that does not bother will raise its score. Many surveys are misleading because of these response problems at the margin. Where numbers are small it is essential to check how many are absent and whether anything was found out about their attainment relative to those who did respond.

The importance of looking carefully at the proportion not responding lies in the possibility that they are not a random sample and may not be similar to those who respond. The interview technique has the advantage that the refusals can be assessed. But in the postal questionnaire, there is no way of knowing whether those who did not reply forgot, were too scared to answer or rugged individualists who would have liked to have told the sender to get lost. There is always the suspicion that the non-responders may have been the most interesting and certainly the most non-conformist group. Thus an attempt in the Authoritarian Personality study to use mailed questionnaires was abandoned, not only because only 20 per cent responded, but because those that did reply were found to be biased in a democratic direction.[24]

Non-response also makes it difficult to interpret generalisations. If 100 out of 200 respond and 90 of these answer YES, does this mean that 90 per cent are in favour or 45 per cent? There is no way of really knowing, although the assumption is usually that those who replied are representative and a huge majority are in favour. But the half who did not reply may have been so violently opposed that they tore up the questionnaire and threw it in the fire.

It is therefore important to look for attempts to anticipate and reduce non-response. Calling back on those who were not in when the interviewer called usually finds a few more. The Government Social Survey insists that it is the duty of an interviewer to call at any time, however inconvenient, or to fix an appointment for a later period to get near a complete response. Even where refusal or failure to contact is finally accepted, there should have been some attempt to assess the characteristics of non-responders. Similarly a follow-up letter with another stamped addressed envelope can bring in more completed forms from a postal questionnaire.

These additions to those responding are not only important in themselves, but can be used to see whether those who cannot be contacted at first or do not reply differ in any systematic way from those responding at first. This is the only way of estimating whether non-responders differ from responders. Thus if it is found that half the people who cannot be contacted in a survey are young married couples, this proportion can be used if it has been decided to bring the number up to that originally intended by additions after failure to contact.

Finally, it must be remembered that non-response occurs only in probability sampling. In purposive samples contacts are made until a quota is filled. The advantages of probability samples are in providing a reliable basis for generalisation and for mathematical calculations. But very often non-response makes a mockery of any complex statistical calculations. It is the way statistics can lend an aura of competence to inadequate samples that makes it essential to find response rates. Studies have been discussed here because they contained these rates. None are therefore as suspect as those in which non-response rates have been omitted.

Theoretical sampling

Glaser and Strauss have encouraged social scientists to pursue theory development through the use of closely observed data. This 'grounded theory' was to be elaborated as observation went on in the case study or ethnography.[25] The theory was to be based in the emerging data and was to guide the collection of more information. This discussion of theory in relation to ethnography has been advanced by recent interest in the UK.[26] Less attention has been paid to the dual interest in observational studies of schools and other institutions. Researchers may be aware of the tension between collecting data for theory elaboration and for describing a situation, but readers are usually left to guess how the former affects the latter.

The first problem in theoretical sampling arises from the need for theory to guide methods. Exampling is inevitable and the influence of preconceptions is likely to increase if the search is for theoretically interesting data. Second, the reader has to accept that the account is not primarily descriptive or representative, but focused on the theoretically interesting. Third, researchers have often found it difficult to detect the data that are theoretically significant.[27] Where this theoretical sampling has been used productively it has been admitted that evidence and interpretation are so run together that the reader has to accept the risk that the researchers substituted their own interpretations of what happened for those of the people studied.[28] Finally, case studies tend to be read for their practical importance rather than their contribution to theory. If the data have been collected because they were relevant to theories about schools as part of the ideological state apparatus, or as arenas for the negotiation of meanings, or about knowledge as control, it should not also be expected to give a valid account of what happens between teachers and pupils. Grounded theory and theoretical sampling increase the chance that the researcher is pressing a case, not just describing it.

TERRORIST OR RESISTANCE FIGHTER? THE CASE OF THE FOOTBALL HOOLIGAN

My contacts with violence on football grounds were divided by the war. My nose was bled at White Hart Lane while unwisely cheering Cliff Bastin as he stroked home a penalty for the great pre-war Arsenal side, and my head was split open by a stray half-brick while spellbound by Benny Fenton at Millwall a decade later. This account of the evidence on football hooliganism is coloured by a personal conviction that life on the terraces has become more peaceful, based on a comparison between Stoke City in the 1970s and London, twenty and thirty years before.

The first major enquiry into football hooliganism was an official report to Denis Howell, then Minister of Sport.[1] This was mainly a questionnaire study. The respondents felt that there was a serious and increasing problem. It led to a working party that suggested many of the crowd control procedures used today. Since the mid-1960s, reports have come in regularly, and most have been based on the assumption that the problem exists and has got worse. Some reports remain at the level of crowd management techniques. Others trace the causes back to declining moral standards generally and to more specific if arguable symptoms of decline such as pop music and violence on television.

It may be however that it is the visibility of the crowd at the popular end, and particularly their audible obscenity that gives the impression of riot. It may be that between 1946 and 1960 there were only 195 cases of disorderly behaviour by spectators notified to the Football Association,[2] but the police were rarely in sight and were not particularly interested when I did point out that half-bricks were falling on my head. Between 1960 and 1966 there were 148 cases. But by the end of that period there were more police about, and most cases were probably reported to the F.A. Public interest had been aroused and may have stimulated the rise in numbers in the statistics, through more reporting of incidents and more sympathetic police response.

There is however another possibility that accounts for the crisis on the football grounds. Public interest is both cause and effect of attention by the mass media. The reporters focus on items of popular interest, but also create or increase that interest. The actual incidence of violence in football grounds is low considering the numbers present, their density and the need to create occasional diversions from the boredom of much that occurs on the park. But the press dramatise it. In Hall's terms, they 'edit for impact'.[3] They can stir up 'moral panics'. Last week football violence this week porn in shop windows, next week glue sniffing in primary schools.

When violence on the terraces is investigated by social scientists even more doubt is thrown on the conventional descriptions of mindlessness or thuggery. Taylor[4] sees the fans as the last of the traditional working class supporters, increasingly alienated by the commercialisation of the game and the clubs. The fan is isolated from his team. Clarke[5] also stresses the importance of changes in the 'people's game'. There is a culture of support, passed on from generation to generation which is violated by recent spectacularisation. Close observation of the fans also illuminates an order about their behaviour and in the way new fans are initiated into the terrace organisation.

There are however conflicting aspects in this evidence. If the problem is created by the media, its analysis, and particularly tracing its historical development is pointless. If it doesn't exist it's getting a lot of attention. If it doesn't exist, it is also painful when it draws blood. If it's to do with the alienation of working class youth from a commercialised game, the passion of Manchester's Red Army supporting a side of Irish and Scots recently recruited to replace local lads at the cost of millions is difficult to explain. Furthermore, it seems strange that such effort should have been given to showing that there is an order among the crowd, when you only have to listen to the chanting to realise that there must be a lot of synchronised if vulgar activity.

It is when the research goes beyond describing behaviour on the terraces to accounting for it, that the evidence becomes contradictory. For Taylor and for Clarke, the factors underlying violence lie in the position of working class youth in modern society. The clue to behaviour lies in the erosion of traditional values right at the league footballing heart of that culture. To Taylor, the lad on the terraces '. . . *has the historic task of perpetuating the traditional values of the fast disappearing football subculture . . .*'[6] But to Marsh, 'aggro', with its ritualistic behaviour, is an outlet for natural aggression. '*Repression of overt expression, coupled with a continued transmission of the aggression process as a central feature of our social fabric*'.[7] Clarke uses the identical historical explanation as Taylor, pointing to the spectacularisation of the game to account for the alienation of the working class fans. From there, Clarke, like Taylor, turns to post-war social conditions. But now it is not a simple reaction against the commercialisation of the game itself, but the physical and social separation of older and younger groups that enables violence to occur, and the need to create excitement and immediacy during the game that accounts for the behaviour behind the goal. Taylor's lads are described as resistance fighters. Marsh sees his boys releasing pent-up aggression, while Clarke sees his football supporters as seeking excitement to compensate for a boring and depressing existence.

As with most of these controversies, there is no way of resolving differences in the analysis of the issue. There are probably elements of all the explanations present, and no doubt many more. In academic courses or discussions, these differences add spice. But when action has to be taken, whether to improve grounds, add to the enjoyment of spectators, including those on the terraces, or keep violence under control, the differences in interpretation do matter, for each leads to different policies. The Joint Sports Council/Social Science Research Council panel on *Public Disorder and Sporting Events*[8] concluded by pointing out several areas where more information was needed, but thought that research had a low priority because it was unlikely to yield much that was useful for action. But Marsh, in a critique of this report, points out that the authors, by searching for solutions, missed the chance of providing a conceptual framework within which recommendations could properly be made. To Marsh, Hall, Clarke and to others interested in the way those on the terraces see the situation, understanding will only come by examining accounts by those involved in the light of the social and political situation in which they find themselves. The dilemma is that while the search for solutions without under-standing is futile, there is no agreement among those who claim to understand.

The lack of agreement among those investigating the causes of violence at football matches is to be expected given the many factors that must be involved. Here social scientists are as far from understanding as the journalists and politicians who press simple solutions to a complex issue. This was well illustrated by the tragedy in the Heysall stadium in 1985. The response ranged from bringing back corporal punishment to confirming another symptom of the decline of Western capitalism. But action had to be taken and the case shows how this does not require understanding. We do not know why people commit crime but we still take action to stop them. We do not know what makes a school effective but we still give advice on how it should be done. We do not know the causes of many diseases but have nevertheless controlled them. There may be many conflicting theories about football violence, but the ad-ministrators of the sport took action to ensure that English fans could not follow their clubs into Europe. Life cannot wait for social research to catch up with it.

5

STUDIES BASED ON OBSERVATION

All research depends on observation. Through the ears and eyes the material and social world is interpreted. But this perception is not passive. Impressions are first selected and then interpreted within the mind of the observer. Between the impression on the senses and the reported interpretation are the attitudes, values and prejudices, as well as the academic conceptual models, of the researcher. Perception is the process of fitting what is seen or heard into these maps and frameworks in the mind.

A psychologist may see a classroom as a situation of organised learning experiences reinforcing correct and inhibiting incorrect answers. A sociologist may see the same scene as a group constrained by the power of the teachers and the interaction of peers. A teacher may see it as a situation to be controlled, a parent as a group affecting their child, a head teacher as a reflection on the competence of the teacher and an inspector as a guide to the efficiency of the school. Individuals enter situations with maps already established in their minds into which they fit the evidence of their senses.

The effect of cultural differences on observation can be gauged from the improbable but delightful contrast between German and American psychologists observing hungry rats confronted by a maze in which food was available at the far end. Both sets of rats learned to traverse the maze. But those seen by the Germans sat pondering the problem in an immobile way until a solution dawned and they threaded their way through. American rats, however, launched themselves hell for leather in a series of bruising trial runs until they learned from their errors. The time taken was similar, the style contrasting. Any student who has puzzled over the differences between gestalt and behaviorist theories of learning will realise that this ludicrous picture reflects an underlying discrepancy due to national differences which seem to have established different frames of reference in the minds of the two national groups which developed these theories.

A more serious if still amusing example of the effects of the expectations of the observer can be demonstrated by Rosenthal and Fode's experiment with twelve psychology students asked to measure the time taken for rats to learn to run to the darker arm of a maze to find food.[1] Sixty ordinary rats were divided between the students, but six students were told they had maze-bright rats and six were given maze-dull rats, each sample said to be specially bred. Each rat was given ten chances each day for five days to learn that the darker arm led to food.

While there was no actual difference in the maze-learning ability of the rats, the students observed the results that they were led to anticipate by the description of their sample as bright or dull. The bright rats not only became better performers but showed daily improvement, while the dull rats only improved to the third day and then deteriorated. Furthermore, the dull rats refused to start at all more frequently than the eager-to-get-with-it bright ones and were slower to reach the end after they had learned. After the experiment was over the students rated their rats and their own attitudes towards them. Those having 'bright' rats viewed them as brighter, more pleasant and more likeable, and their own attitude towards the rats was more relaxed and enthusiastic than among the six students with the 'dull' sample.

Such effects are not confined to the social sciences, although the frequent use of human beings as subjects of research makes them more prone to self-fulfilling effects. In the natural sciences a researcher can be similarly misled, either by the expectations of colleagues or his own predictions and hopes. Once set to expect a result, a scientist in all fields is liable to find his observations biased. This is why controls and repetitions of experiments by others are so important.

The case of Prosper Blondlot and his discovery of *n*-rays reported in Chapter 1 is a typical example. At the heart of his spectroscopic apparatus was a prism. This was removed by the American physicist Robert Wood, unnoticed by Blondlot, who continued his descriptions of the *n*-rays he was observing, despite the absence of the lens that was supposed to produce them. It was not however just the inventor who saw what he expected to see. Other French scientists were similarly deceiving themselves at this time when new rays were eagerly anticipated.

Styles of observation

Observation is the basic technique for researchers. It is also most likely to be affected by personal, professional and political views. Hence there are difficult decisions at the start of research about the degree to which observations are to be controlled or left free-ranging and whether the style is to be participant or detached. Detached observation is possible as in the use of schedules such as that developed by Bales.[2] Small groups, in specially designed rooms, were observed by specially trained observers sitting behind one-way mirrors. Adaptations of this method were used in the ORACLE project.[3] The aim is to maximise reliability by training observers to sample events systematically and stick to the categories of behaviour listed on the schedule.

As the interest in the interpretation of human behaviour has increased, detached and controlled observation has become unpopular. If you are after the meaning of events to those involved, you need to be more like Sherlock Holmes, exercising ingenuity, than Inspector Lestrade following the book. That is the message of Chapter 3. Those who want to interpret social affairs try not to upset the natural setting, and design and redesign their research as new data are collected and stay alert for theories that explain it. Participant observation is the dominant style because it gives the required flexibility.

The complete participant observer merges into the groups studied. Homan blends into the Pentacostal groups he is studying[4] as do the sociology students observing what happens *When Prophecy Fails* reported later.[5] In education that isn't so easy. Thus Davies in her *Life in the Classroom and Playground* is very concerned with the difficulties of really getting to know how children give meaning to events. Adult researchers may think they have found out, but the culture of childhood is well defended.[6] Thus even those researchers who observe while taking the role of teacher may become part of the normal life of the school, but get no nearer the real world of the children. Indeed, the participant role that is chosen to preserve the natural situation may even reduce the chance of finding out what the pupils really think.

It is not easy to illustrate bias in observational studies because replication is not easy. The group or its environment will have changed across time. The participation of a different observer may have its effect. Replication is in any case rare. However, in 1951, Oscar Lewis published his *Life in a Mexican Village: Tepoztlan Revisited.*[7] This was a study of communities previously studied by Redfield in the 1930s.[8] Redfield had seen Tepoztlan as a society in which there was little change, a strong sense of belonging together and a homogeneity among the inhabitants. Lewis, in re-studying the community, was not trying to prove Redfield wrong, but looking for the type of errors that could be made in community studies. To Lewis, Tepoztlan manifested individualism not cooperation, tensions, fear and distrust rather than Redfield's picture of contentment and a sense of community. Later, in 1969, Avila published another study of this area of Mexico and again refuted the view that change was slow or the people uncompetitive.[9]

It may be that the community had genuinely changed over the period from the 1930s to the 1950s and 1960s. But it may have been that Redfield saw information that fitted into the folk-urban continuum that was his theoretical model. The hypothesis may have directed the observations. Redfield later tried to explain the differences between himself and Lewis.[10] He points out that both he and Lewis would have brought their own views into their work, and would have been alerted to see activity that confirmed their very different positions on urban and rural life. Once again this is an illustration of the way 'facts' are created by reference to theory. Where the theories differ, so may the 'facts'.

There are now several accounts of experiences of participant observers in education collected by Burgess.[11] These confirm that participant observation troubles researchers. Some forty researchers in these three books expose their concern over reliability and validity. It is an insight not readily available to the reader of the original books and articles, for these only contain brief sections on method. It is not just anxiety over which role to adopt, complete participant, participant-as-observer, observer-as-participant or complete observer, or about their effect on those observed, but about the impact on them. Social scientists enter the field alerted by theories and models. But reality is often a shock and the models often do not fit.

Seeley working in an American community describes his experiences as a loss of innocence.[12] His sociology came to be seen as a shared illusion unrelated to the reality he experienced. Similarly, Stein finds that to get insight into his community means detaching himself from his subject.[13] Wolff, going south of the border in Mexico, uses the term 'surrender' to describe the way he became and had to become, immersed in the community he wished to understand.[14] The development of interpretive social science has helped prepare for such experiences. Indeed, it was the experiences of sociologists such as Seeley, Stein and Wolff that pushed the subject away from its scientistic stance. But the shock is still felt once you get in a school, a community or anywhere outside academia. Life out there is often beyond rationalisation in a model.

There is also a serious ethical problem if researchers 'pass' themselves off as bread roundsmen (Ditton),[15] gang members (Patrick)[16] or watchqueen (Humphreys),[17] in order to get into natural situations. This also raises problems for the reader of the published accounts of the deception. They have to be taken on trust and because each publication makes it less likely that the deception can be repeated, the chances of confirmation or refutation are diminished. The report may have all the veracity as well as the intimacy of a Peeping Tom's notebook.

This issue is complicated by the dilemma that the scientist is in if he starts observing without the consent of the observed or by clandestine means. He is nevertheless a scientist committed to report what he finds and not to conceal information or distort it to protect his informants. This dilemma can be followed in the work of Whyte on street corner gangs.[18] Here it was a combination of respect for those who had befriended him and provided the information, coupled with a fear that adverse accounts of them would put the author in danger of being carved up. Whyte's study lasted four years. By the end he was playing an active part in Cornerville society. To his informants he was writing a book. He visited them after publication to gauge its impact. Perhaps this is an indication of the compromise nature of the book. Nevertheless it remains a classic, and its methodological appendix has a full discussion of the ethical issues.

Probably the most fascinating but most morally dubious study was Festinger, Riecken and Schachter's *When Prophecy Fails*.[19] Here the authors and their students infiltrated a group who had prophesied that the end of the world was nigh. The social scientists were fully accepted and even after the world carried on passed its predicted end, another observer was introduced to check on the impact of this miscalculation on the group. Recording was done in the toilet, out on the porch or on midget tape recorders. This was an extreme example, but most social scientists have experienced moments when they have access to information that is obviously private. Publish and be damned can be justified on scientific grounds, but a public conned once is unlikely to cooperate again. Furthermore, social scientists are not exempt from the responsibility to exercise power over others with restraint.

WHAT DO SCHOOL LEAVERS THINK ABOUT SCHOOLS?

The difficulty in arriving at reliable, valid and generalisable evidence can be best illustrated by looking at research dealing with an apparently simple question. How do teenagers leaving school look back on their schooling? Obviously there will be differences between groups of children, in different types of school, in different areas, but it should not be too difficult to select a group of, say, unskilled workers' children, from one type of school such as comprehensive, in an area such as the inner city, and to question them about their experiences and attitudes. In case there is a gap between what they say and do, the questions could be supplemented by entering schools and observing actual behaviour.

When the concern is with factual questions such as the subjects that were liked or disliked, researchers have come up with similar results for similar children. But when attitudes towards school have been investigated there has been little agreement in the evidence. In 1973, two researchers, Willis[1] in the Midlands and Scharff[2] in London, were independently looking at the same issue, transition from school to work. Each looked at working class children. The selected schools in both cases were comprehensives grown out of secondary moderns. Both worked in inner cities and all the schools had a sizeable number of black children in their intakes. Both researchers worked intensively in the schools, observing, asking questions in an unstructured, informal way, getting to know the teenagers and concentrating on their attitudes and behaviour as they prepared to leave school and enter work. In both accounts of the work the text is illustrated by quotes in the language of the children.

There is evidence from these two studies that is similar. The teachers in both areas were concerned, yet worried. The careers service is criticised in both. But the rest of the evidence presented from these two very similar studies of the same phenomena show schools that belong to different worlds. Anyone reading these two books for a description of contemporary schooling would face apparently completely conflicting evidence.

To Willis, 'The most basic, obvious and explicit dimension of counter-school culture is entrenched general and personalised opposition to "authority".'[3] The twelve lads studied made life a misery for the teachers. They were scornful of their studious peers. They opposed all that the teachers supported. The quotes from these teenagers are peppered with 'fucking' this and 'fucking' that. The teachers concerned survived only by avoiding having to maintain order. This was achieved by using discovery and individualised learning techniques to avoid overt conflict in the classroom.

There is nothing very surprising about this picture. The punch in this research of Willis is in his explanation of the way the evidence accounts for the way working class kids get working class jobs, and accept this destiny. To Willis, it is the children's own culture, own response to schooling, that prepares them for manual labour. They damn themselves into taking subordinate roles at work through their opposition to their schooling. This group may be a minority, and generalisation should be cautious, but it is a brilliant and sobering message.

However, at the same time, in similar schools, in similar urban conditions, with the same aged children, only a hundred miles to the south, Scharff, using similar methods, was reaching very different conclusions. Scharff's adolescents also seemed resistant and resentful. They also seemed to be angry. But these teenagers actually wanted to get closer to their teachers. They were willing to cooperate. In their quotes there are no four letter words. Furthermore, their anger, their surly behaviour and their protests against schooling are interpreted as symptoms of the numbness, disbelief, sense of loss felt at having to leave the school, which, deep down, is felt to be a 'mothering institution'. The teenagers here were 'mourning' their loss and responded by denying the value of their schooling.[4]

Here is a strange contrast. Was the difference due to the selection of very different samples, one totally counter-cultural, the other totally mainstream-cultural? There is no way of knowing. Was Willis mistaken? Was that resistance to teachers really covering up the impending loss of contact with the school? Or was Scharff mistaken? Was that cooperation really covering up some profound aspect of a capitalist society? Superficially both explanations are possible. Willis examines the structure of capitalism to explain what happens in the transition from school to work. Scharff derives his explanation from an examination of human emotions at times of transition such as leaving school and entering work.

What would have happened if Scharff had looked at the lads in the Midlands? All that resentment might have been a way of concealing a genuine attachment to the school. Willis may have been misled into believing that what was said and done reflected the real selves of these teenagers. What would have happened if Willis had looked at the teenagers in London? Would those same cooperative, genteel-speaking children have been seen as subversive and foul-mouthed? It is not likely that he would have seen manifestations of mourning the loss of the school on leaving. He would probably have seen a society where a sizeable minority have only the prospect of a dead-end job and where schools perform the cooling-down of ambition that prevents revolution and even protest, and which actually ensures that the lads look forward to their future in manual labour.

By now the unfairness of these contrasts will be clear to readers who are in a position to detect that Scharff is a psychiatrist and Willis a sociologist. They may have been looking at similar situations. But each was trained in a different discipline. Each was alerted by professional practice to see different aspects of behaviour and to hear different words. Each would interpret the same data in different ways. These authors would also have had different political outlooks. Both have given accounts that may have been valid in their terms, within their theoretical frameworks. The transition from school to work may involve both mourning for the school and hatred of the school. Each could occur in the same teenager. But the unwary reader of only one of these books would get a very one-sided view of working class attitudes to school. The lay reader of both would be justifiably confused. Only when the discipline from which the researcher operates is known can the account be evaluated and the four key questions in the Foreword answered.

This work on school leavers is typical in dealing with boys only. In 1979, however, work started on a Social Science Research Council-funded project on the transition to work of young, working-class women. This was directed by Griffin, working at the Centre for Contemporary Cultural Studies alongside Willis.[5] This study employed quantitative and qualitative methods. Griffin found that the young women did not fit into the pro- and anti-school groupings identified by Willis. The young women did not go around in gangs, but joined in close friendships with two or three friends and changed these frequently. Here the problems within schools were not seen as the degree of aggressive disruption, but of uncontrolled sexuality. But it was less the results of the research that were surprising than the impact of researching girls rather than boys. Griffin was assumed to be a feminist simply because she was looking into young women leaving school.

6

INFORMATION THROUGH ASKING QUESTIONS

If you want an answer, ask a question. Whether it is an attempt to reconstruct the past, describe the present or predict the future, the questionnaire and the interview have come to dominate the collection of information in the social sciences, particularly sociology. Yet, 'When did you last ...?', 'How many times did you ...?' and 'How will you ...?' are questions that will not just produce answers but will reconstruct the meaning of the situation in which the asker and answerer are involved. The asking of questions is the main source of social scientific information about everyday behaviour, yet between question and answer there may be shifts in the relation between scientist and subject. The final answers emerge from this interaction and the meanings that each party gives to the situation. The questions have created this situation and the answers are meaningful only in its context.

Asking questions to get valid answers is therefore a skilled and sensitive job requiring knowledge of the environment in which the questionnaire is to be filled in or the interview conducted. It requires knowledge of the likely impact of questioner on respondent. It requires a sensitivity to the symbolic sophistication of humans, non-verbal as well as verbal. Imagine, with Jowell and Hoinville, a poll conducted among coloured immigrants to discover their attitudes towards subsidised repatriation to their country of origin shortly after a speech by Enoch Powell.[1] Such a poll for Panorama by Opinion Research Centre asked such questions as 'Would you like to return to your country of origin if you received financial help?' Asked this way a majority might be expected to say 'yes'. But now imagine the question being asked by white, middle-class, middled-aged women interviewers, on a rainy, cold day in late

November in the middle of the Black Country. To anyone even capable of envisaging Trinidad or Jamaica the answers 'Yes', 'No', or 'Don't know' are more likely to have meant 'Yes please', 'Get lost' or 'How much!' A thought about the interaction and shifting of ground that was likely to have occurred in those macabre interviews should say more than any interactionist treatise.

There is a whole spectrum of situations in the use of questionnaires and interviews, ranging from the postal questionnaire where there is no direct contact, to the psychoanalyst's couch where there is much. The same problems are present as in observational studies, particularly those of the degree of control and the amount of interaction. The postal questionnaire is not exempt. A parallel is the filling in of an income tax return and its interpretation by the Inland Revenue Inspector. The difficulty of the public in filling in a form designed for simplicity, the problems of the Inspector in sorting out genuine from bogus claims and the general puzzling out of how the other party responded or will respond to the questions and answers gives a good idea of the design difficulties and the interaction, even when there has been no personal contact.

There is, however, the extra factor in the interview of the two personalities involved. Interaction now is not only structured by the questions, but by personal feelings. The choice between questionnaires and interviews is usually determined by the high cost of the latter, but it is, once again, also a choice between reliability and insight. Adjustments can be made in interviews and answers can be probed. The cost is in reliability, for if the same interview was done by another interviewer the chance of identical results would usually be low. Agencies like the Government Social Survey obtain high reliability by sticking to set questions and probes, but few organisations are so scrupulous, few studies lend themselves to such rigid questions and there is always the effect of non-verbal clues intervening.

A tale by Blackburn serves to illustrate the need for caution over the validity and permanence of answers from questions.[2] A month after the publication of the influential and carefully designed study of affluent workers at Vauxhalls in Luton, maintaining that 77 per cent of workers were contented with management and working conditions, there was an open revolt with the singing of the Red

Flag, a storming of management offices and threats of lynching the directors. The opinions expressed in answer to questions may be short-lived and shallow, but once written into articles and books, or incorporated into lectures they acquire a permanence that belies their actual instability. There are quick profits to be made from questionnaires. Productivity can be boosted by the use of computers. The consumer needs the protection of a few basic guides to quality.

Was there a pilot study?

Whenever questions are to be asked and a choice made from a limited list of answers it is a safeguard if they are tried out in advance. This is a way to avoid many of the mistakes described in the rest of this chapter. The trial run checks that the questions are feasible for the sample. Pilot studies are essential for ensuring that the responses offered as possible answers actually do exhaust all the possibilities. Only by giving a free choice at this stage can all the possible answers be gauged. Some questions may be found useless as the range of answers will be limitless. Others will be found to force similar choices on everyone. Others will be beyond the understanding of the sample. Others will be greeted with derision.

Ideally the answers offered should exhaust all the possibilities and not overlap with each other. In practice respondents often find it difficult to choose an answer that fits their views. Similarly the 'don't know' answer may be found to be used not only by the ignorant, but by those who can not find an answer that fits their attitudes. This type of feasibility study in advance usually combines a check on possible questions with free-ranging unstructured questions allowing the pilot sample to give their own views on the subject under study. In some cases the open-ended enquiry may form a first pilot study and the actual testing of questions a second stage. Without any pilot stage, the actual research is likely to address unsuitable questions to bewildered people.

How long was it?

A skilled interviewer may be able to sustain interest and cooperation through a long session. Sessions of six to eight hours

have been achieved.[3] At the other extreme, long postal questionnaires are probably never the basis of published work as not even
the usual 30 per cent survive the wastepaper basket. The actual
length depends on the nature of the sample and the motivation
created by the topic. The span of attention of children increases
only slowly with age. Old people tire easily. Head teachers, business
men and upper middle class are impatient with any form that may
be time-wasting. The span of interest may increase with education
but so does scepticism.

How difficult were the questions?

Questions can be too technical or complex. Payne reports trick
questions producing support for fictitious Acts and even obtained a
substantial percentage in favour of incest.[4] People are wary of
admitting ignorance of an issue. The slightest clue will then be used
as a guide to an answer. Some words have no precise meaning. The
establishment, democracy and big business can raise emotions but
obscure issues. 'Fair' is not an alternative answer to 'good' or 'bad',
as it has many meanings. The author was once alerted to a survey
that indicated an alarming increase in spirit-drinking among
schoolchildren. The university department concerned had found
many children going to the toilets for a whisky. Fortunately this was
corrected before publication as all the teachers concerned knew that
this was local slang for masturbation. Once again there is the
tendency for social scientists to impose their definitions on terms
which have their own everyday meaning.

Even when words are straightforward, they can form a question
that can baffle the public. In long questions asking for a choice
between alternatives, the last is more often chosen because the first
has been forgotten. A good criterion if the actual questions are
available in the article or book is to check that they can be
understood. The author should not be given the benefit of the
doubt. Here for example is a question from a survey of knowledge
about English language skills designed by Morris and reported to
the World Congress on Reading in 1986.[5]

> 'Please give first the comparative form and then the superlative form
> beside each adjective:
> Fat, fine, sly, bad, tall, good, rough, merry, beautiful, curious'.

The author found the results 'frightening'. Only 18 per cent of the students could write down the comparatives and superlatives. But later contributors to the *Times Educational Supplement* pointed to what should have been obvious to Morris.[6] Student teachers do not use the words 'baddest' or 'gooder'. They were either having a laugh at the expense of the researcher or confused, quite understandably, by the question. The conclusion drawn was that the researcher not the teachers of English should examine her expertise.

Could the questions have suggested the answers?

It is not so much that leading questions are deliberately used, but that it is very difficult not to use them. This is why groups for or against legal abortion, the Common Market, capital punishment, blood sports and the Sunday opening of Welsh pubs can produce convincing evidence to support their case by taking to the streets with a questionnaire. This is rarely dishonesty. It is sometimes technical incompetence. It is often innocence of the ease with which questions can be asked to get the results that are wanted.

The following question was the basis of an article maintaining that large numbers of reluctant teachers were entering colleges of education.[7] 'If you were quite free to choose, and could obtain the qualifications necessary, what field of employment would you ideally like to enter?' Fifty-three per cent of the students in colleges of education to whom this question was put indicated some profession other than teaching. Yet given the nature of the question it is remarkable that any opted for teaching. It is not known whether any other professional group would have this or any other degree of commitment for the authors did not provide this basis for comparison.

Was prestige or emotion involved?

Advertisers exploit the ease with which people can be led to associate themselves with the prestigeful. All the best people soak their teeth overnight in X after seducing their girl friend with gin and Y tonic. It may not seem decent to admit that the wogs begin at

Boulogne and it is better to say you read the *Spectator* than *Pu...*
Questions can easily lead people to choose right not real answers.
Furthermore, there may always be a reluctance to use the 'don't
know' category. None of us likes to be made to seem ignorant,
especially about an issue that the man with the schedule obviously
thinks important.

Could the environment have influenced the answers?

Where questions are asked about life in schools, old people's homes,
prisons or other relatively closed organisations, there may be
pressure to give answers within a particular context. Again right not
real answers appear. The author, comparing responses from the
same students on questionnaires and interviews in a college of
education, had to scrap the use of unverified questionnaires because
students were giving the answers they thought students in training
should give.[8] Only when group discussions were held to examine
the discrepancy in answers was this innocent deception uncovered.
Yet combinations of methods facilitating such cross-checking are
rare. Usually a single instrument is considered enough.

When were answers pre-coded?

Questions can be unstructured, giving the respondent a free rein to
answer at will, or structured, giving him only a choice of answers
listed by the researcher. In the first case the researcher takes the
answers and sorts them out into categories after collection. In the
latter type this categorisation is done before the start of data
collection. In both cases the researcher is imposing his social
scientific framework around the possible common sense answers of
his respondents. There is rarely a perfect fit. There is usually a
pruning and bending to make the irregular everyday responses fit
into the categories prepared for them. This happens in both
sequences. But leaving the categorisation to the end by using open-
ended, unstructured questions leaves a lot to the discretion of the
researcher or his coding staff, and this particular Procrustean bed is
hidden from the reader.

/ depend on the quality of the questions asked,
.ess of, and control over, the interaction involved.
.an be more flexible than the questionnaire, it can
, can be adjusted to circumstances, can increase
.ooperation. But the cost may be a reduction in control
anు ,uently in reliability. As these issues are discussed in the
followin₅ pages, it must be remembered that there is always
interaction involved in the filling in of questionnaires.

The way clues can be incidentally presented and skilfully
interpreted can be gauged from Pfungst's investigation of Clever
Hans, a horse that could apparently solve mathematical problems,
spell and identify musical notes by nodding his head, tapping his
feet or pointing to letters on a board.[9] Public and experts were
baffled and his master, Van Osten, a schoolmaster, made no profit
from the act. Pfungst, by diligently controlling factors in the
environment of the performance, found that although Clever Hans
could answer even when the question was not even spoken, the
questioner had to be present and seen by the horse. He noticed how
tense the questioner got as the horse appeared to start to tap or point
to the right answer. Pfungst now saw what all animal trainers rely
on, that the horse could detect these slight involuntary clues.
Pfungst even learned the trick himself so that, on all fours and
blindfolded, he could answer questions from his audience without
them being spoken. If a horse can detect the muscular movements
as clues, man, the symbol-using animal must respond to much more
than mere questions in an interview situation.

If the reader can get past the substance of the Kinsey Reports to
the sections on method, they will find an acid test of interviewing.[10]
It was necessary to stop any tendency to brag or distort as the
sample were volunteers. Many indeed seemed to want to measure
their sexual prowess against others. Complete confidentiality,
absolute privacy during interviewing and no suggestions of right
and wrong behaviour were the guides to rapport. Kinsey himself
carried out 7,000 interviews lasting an hour to an hour and a half.
This labour of love was conducted deadpan; friendly, but never
with any expression of surprise or disapproval.

The questions were asked as directly as possible to avoid

interaction. The interviewer looked squarely at the subject and moved inexorably from factual background to intimate detail. Questions were fired rapidly, giving little time to think. Frank sexual terms were used. When abnormal behaviour was being probed it was 'How many times?', not 'Do you . . .?' Questions were used to check others, husbands were checked against wives, reinterviewing after eighteen months was employed. This study is acknowledged as classic. Its weaknesses are in its sampling rather than the method of interviewing. It is important, however, to remember that the questions were about actual sexual behaviour not attitudes towards it. The reports give little salacious pleasure and are a reliable guide for the same reasons.

Were the interviewers trained?

Kinsey and his three associates memorised the coding system of their interview schedules so that subjects saw only symbols being recorded. Most reputable research agencies have some form of selection and training programmes for their interviewers. The Government Social Survey uses only standardised, structured interviews. Because design is by experts and questions are piloted, the interviewers have to follow the wording of the schedules. Some latitude is allowed over factual questions, but with attitude questions there can be repetition but no alteration. Even prompts are written into the schedules and stock phrases are provided for probing obscure answers.[11]

Obviously with such care over design and such control over the interviewers, training is necessary. Moser reports that only 16 per cent of applicants finally passed all tests and went on to actual training in 1953.[12] Applicants are sent a handbook to study in advance and invited to attend a three-day initial training class. Those accepted after this go into the field with a training officer who demonstrates the method and observes early attempts. If successful a probationary period is entered during which supervision is provided. Then a written test is given on the principles in the handbook. Trial interviews are recorded to check reliability. Even when fully trained and experienced there is still supervision by training officers. Once on the job these interviewers know how to approach subjects, how and where to sit, the tone of the voice to use and the time to bring out the schedules.

Government Social Survey workers have to be particular because of the importance of the subject matter they handle. But this care illustrates the gap between the best and the worst. Many market research organisations have no selection procedures and little training. It is common to use students from social science departments both as training for them and as ways of gathering data for research. Anyone who has interviewed, canvassed or even tried to get factual information from strangers knows that the apparent incomprehension of many people is boundless. In addition the interaction can range from hostility, through indifference to seduction. Training at least alerts the innocent.

The success of training has been illustrated by Durbin and Stuart.[13] Here experienced Government Social Survey and experienced British Institute of Public Opinion interviewers were compared with another sample of inexperienced students. There was a striking and consistent difference in the proportion of schedules that were successfully completed. The experienced got more filled in, received fewer refusals, and reported fewer 'gone away'.

Who was being interviewed?

It has already been suggested that interviewing within organisations might be affected by particular circumstances, making generalisations hazardous. But other groups are likely to respond to interviewers in ways that introduce bias. Rich has pointed to the authority of an adult when interviewing children.[14] The child will be likely to seize on an answer rather than telling the whole truth. To Holt, a child's response to teaching is usually a game to deceive by acting docile, looking attentive, acting silly and so on.[15] If skilled teachers are fooled, interviewers will have little chance of learning the game. This is especially the case with difficult questions where children are reluctant to answer 'don't know' and will grab at any hints offered. Part of the skill of being a pupil is to be able to detect clues and give the answer the adult wants even though it was not understood. Another difficulty is in communication. To phrase questions in words understandable by children is difficult, and there is a tendency to try to overcome this by speaking to them as if they were rather dense foreigners, thus further increasing the artificiality of the situation and the motive of the child to play the game this apparently simple-minded interviewer wants.

Old people are similarly prone to grab at answers and to answer irrelevantly.[16] They are also liable to grab the interviewer and involve him in some personal gossip. The interviewer is often someone to talk to, or from whom to get advice or sympathy. The interviewer struggles to get his question in against the old person's attempt to introduce his own problems. The old, like the young, are not likely to tell the interviewer to push off but are likely to suck him into their own personal world. In these cases the danger in the impact of everyday and scientific constructions of reality is that the former will engulf the latter, leaving the interviewer with the job of making some sense of the data in his terms once he has escaped from his subject.

The interaction that links questions and answers

The questionnaire and the interview involve interaction between researcher and respondent. The interaction ranges from the impersonal postal questionnaire, to the intimate, unstructured interview. But in every case there is a meeting of different definitions of the same situation, whether the respondents are willing or reluctant. Given the majority who dispose of postal questionnaires into the waste bin, it can be assumed that many who agree to be interviewed do so with reluctance. The answers received will be affected by this interaction as well as by the questions asked.

The choice of methods of asking questions is not only determined by the researcher's concern to get beneath surface responses to the meanings given to situations. Clearly there would be no point in using unstructured interviews for the Census, nor in trying to use postal questionnaires in a study of fiddling at work. The researcher makes a choice after considering the cost, the resources available, the time in which the data has to be collected, as well as the subject matter and the likely balance of reliability and validity. There may be occasions when a questionnaire, because it reduces interaction, may obtain more valid results than an interview. Kinsey's brisk interviewing style probably obtained more valid results than would some more intimate tête à tête over sexual behaviour.[17] There is a general guide that the unstructured interview is probably the most informative, but in the hands of the unskilled is liable to be the most disastrous.[18] The structured interview is safer for the amateur. Similarly, an unwary or unscrupulous researcher can extract any information desired from an unstructured questionnaire, but less damage is likely through biased interpretation when the questions are tightly structured. Facilitating interaction increases the chance of validity, but makes it more difficult to obtain reliability.

The interview and the questionnaire are the most important means of collecting information in the social sciences. The methodological problems in their use also lie at the centre of the differences between those who focus primarily on behaviour and those who look first at the meanings given to events by those involved. The use of structured questionnaires and interviews is opposed by the latter because they are the means of imposing meanings on respondents. They inhibit the use of just the taken-for-granted, everyday terms that those concerned with understanding how people make sense of the world are looking for. Similarly the training of interviewers is a way of ensuring that the imposed structure remains intact. Even probes to produce answers when the respondent does not reply are seen as further instruments for imposing the researcher's interpretation of the situation on those being studied. Because there is interaction in the interview or when filling in a questionnaire, the positivist imposes preconceived categories and terms. Because that imposition inhibits the production of everyday interpretations, concepts and language, the social phenomenologist or symbolic interactionist sees it resulting in a deceptive, bogus objectivity.

In practice, researchers who know their trade are aware of the dangers of distortion through structuring and of unreliabilty through lack of structure. Thus J. and E. Newson, investigating the sensitive area of child-rearing, used the interview to get information from the mother, in her home.[19] They developed a technique that created an unrestrained climate in which the mother would talk freely about her child. What the mother said was seen as important. The tape-recorder was used as a way in which this climate could be retained; it enabled the interviewer to give all her attention to the mother. Because there was no need to write down the significant contributions from the mothers they were less inhibited. But information was pencilled into the interview schedules to limit the time needed to transcribe the tapes later on. They describe this sensitive interviewing as an art form. There must be a genuine interest in the responses given so that the interviewer as expert still retains a natural, unforced interview situation. Here the interview was being used to gather information in an area important for public policy. The problems revolving around control and spontaneity at the theoretical level were thought through in the Newson's work as a result of the practical situation faced. There is nothing surprising in this coincidence of theoretical and practical concern. Asking questions and getting answers involves interaction. The nature of that interaction is at the heart of sociology and social psychology. But it is also a central concern of researchers involved in producing evidence to affect policy. In both cases a balance is being sought between reliability through control and validity through spontaneity.

TO STREAM OR UNSTREAM?

This controversy illustrates the difficulty of obtaining conclusive answers to practical problems through research, even where the design problems appear to be small. But it also shows how evidence can be interpreted to present a case which is more formidable than warranted.

In the 1930s streaming was introduced into most elementary schools. This grouping by ability was soon supported by evidence from educational psychology. The attack on streaming opened in the 1950s. This was part of a general attack on selection procedures, secondary organisation as well as streaming. It has been notable for the vigour and organisation of the parties involved. It soon stimulated a movement in defence of the established system, making it difficult for the lay reader, not knowing the allegiance of the writer, to judge the reliability of the evidence used. Only in 1970 was a large-scale, adequately controlled and neutral investigation published.[1] It was predictably inconclusive.

The first campaign for de-streaming opened in the magazine *Forum*. De-streaming soon became a popular research topic. The first evidence came from Finch (1954),[2] Rudd (1956),[3] Blandford (1958),[4] Morris (1959),[5] and Daniels (1959).[6] Finch, Blandford and Daniels favoured de-streaming. Morris found streaming beneficial for the teaching of reading and Rudd detected little difference in the two methods. In 1959 Yates and Pidgeon from the neutral position of the National Foundation cautioned readers about drawing conclusions from these early and poorly controlled studies.[7]

The zenith of the reformers came in 1964. *Forum* held a conference, submitted evidence to the Plowden committee and published a paperback, *Non-Streaming in the Junior School*.[8] In this year Douglas published *The Home and the School* reporting that streaming reinforced social selection within the schools.[9] Finally Jackson condemned streaming as discriminatory and unjust.[10] The shortcomings of the Douglas study have already been discussed. Jackson drew extensively on Daniels and used personal interpretation rather than detached investigation as a method.

Only after 1964 was the attitude of the teachers controlled in the experiments. In the Plowden Report streaming was shown to lead to higher attainment. De-streaming was favoured, but only if the attitudes of teachers and the organisation of learning were favourable. Finally in 1970 a major study for the National Foundation for Educational Research was published.[11] Here 5,500 children in seventy-two junior schools were studied. With the controls built into this research no clear conclusions were drawn. Given enthusiastic, skilful teachers, non-streaming had advantages, particularly for the motivation of children. But even in unstreamed schools about half the teachers still supported streaming. Increased control over this influence had here led to decreased certainty.

This tendency for reliability and certainty to be inversely proportional appears in all the major studies. In the USA, not only is the most carefully controlled experiment inconclusive,[12] but a review of all available American research could also detect nothing definite.[13] In Sweden a summary of the available investigations suggested that streaming produced slightly better results in academic achievement.[14] Finally a review of evidence from many countries concluded that streaming could not be explained in solely educational terms, but was essentially a reflection of the organisation of society.[15] This review of international evidence also concluded that conclusive evidence was unlikely ever to be collected as the variables involved were too complicated for adequate control. The attitude of the teachers was the most important and the most difficult to control. It was also the link between the organisation of the society and the organisation of learning.

The failure to produce conclusive evidence over a method of organising schoolchildren where controlled experiment is possible and the subjects unlikely to distort the results deliberately indicates the limits of social scientific research as a reliable source for decision-making. Few areas of research present such an apparently simple design problem. Yet the efforts of researchers in many countries to improve design to answer the question of streaming or non-streaming have only led to greater certainty that the results will be inconclusive.

This is not the impression given to students or the lay public. The research has been used as a weapon, not a flashlight. It took twenty years in England for a major study to be published after the start of a campaign backed by small-scale research. Excluding the cautious evidence of Douglas, the accounts appearing in books are heavily selective. Of all the small-scale studies, the most quoted is that of Daniels, which was also the most favourable towards de-streaming. Indeed, no other research has produced such strong evidence for the academic as well as the social benefits of de-streaming. This is the one higher degree thesis which is extensively quoted by students in examination answers. Yet this was only a pioneering study by an enthusiastic egalitarian of two pairs of junior schools with negligible controls. The conclusions about the brighter and duller children were inevitably based on very few children. It is significant that Daniel's study was chosen for replication by the Surrey Educational Research Association.[16] The report, published in 1968, came to the opposite conclusions. Here achievement in streamed schools was significantly higher. The same methods produced opposite results.

It is easy to be too dismissive of this research to establish whether streaming is beneficial or harmful. The inconclusiveness of the comparisons between streamed and unstreamed classes is itself important. It confirms that no single organisational change is going to make all that difference. It dampens down the protagonists. Particularly in the case of the Barker Lunn study it brings out the importance of the attitudes of teachers. If they are luke-warm, de-streaming is unlikely to work. The confirmation of the importance of this evidence, however disappointing it is not to show conclusively that de-streaming is a disaster or a success, lies in the response to Barker Lunn's research.[17] The evidence may have been neutral, but 'streamers' and 'non-streamers' attacked it with equal vigour. The function of social research is often to show that human organisation is rarely all good or bad, but dependent on many complicated factors. It is important to check the over-simplification of human issues.

Further studies by the National Foundation for Educational Research have confirmed this conclusion that streaming is unlikely to have a marked impact on attainment independent of the support of the teachers.[18] This is confirmed by the quasi experiment[18] at Banbury School in the 1970s.[19] Here children were allocated to 'halls', some streamed, some unstreamed. Thus a natural experimental situation existed. But once again the grouping used had little effect compared with other factors such as the primary school from which the children had come. Researchers go on trying to find differences in attainment between mixed ability grouping and streaming because it is an important issue and because it seems so easy to set the experiment up. But once there is sufficient control neither form of grouping seems superior. It's frustrating but realistic. No single factor is going to affect attainment dramatically.

The English research into the effectiveness of different forms of classroom organisation is only a small part of an international effort. In a review of this evidence from the USA, Sweden, Israel and the UK in particular, Dar and Resh[20] confirm that the apparently straightforward question of whether to group or mix by ability cannot be answered without considering factors inside and outside the school. This may be frustrating for those seeking the key to instant success, but is realistic. It is unlikely that any organisation of learning is going to be superior or inferior for all children, at all times, in all schools, for all subjects. Learning is more likely to be specific to the characteristics of the learners, the teachers, the topics and the context of learning. The more we know about learning and its organisation, the cruder becomes the question 'to stream or unstream?'

7

EXPERIMENTS

Experimentation is central to science because researchers have control over factors affecting the event in which they are interested. Thus one or more factors, the independent variables, can be manipulated, while others are controlled, in order to observe the impact of the manipulation on one or more other factors, the dependent variables. The method can range from examining simple relations, say the effects of introducing random register checks on school attendance while controlling for other factors such as time in the week, age of children or the weather, to examining the relations of one set of variables such as those involved in the organisation of schooling to another set, for example, indicators of outputs from schooling. The common element in experimentation is that control is exercised over variables to maximise reliability. The cost of control is often to reduce validity as the situation can be reduced to artificiality.

There are few possibilities for experimentation on humans. Even in education, which is really a large-scale experiment in controlling behaviour to produce results, the degree of control has to be restricted. Social engineering is discouraged. Thus, most experimentation in the social sciences depends on compromising over control. In education it means comparisons between methods of teaching, or curriculum, or organisation that are already in place and cannot be disturbed. This is quasi experimentation. Another method is to control statistically, usually through correlational experimentation. A third is to trace factors back into the past to account for current situations, which is *ex post facto* experimentation.

The diagram shows the simplest experimental design. It starts with random assignment to the experimental or the control group. That assignment controls all the independent variables, providing the numbers allocated are large enough.

	Observation	Intervention	Observation
Experimental sample	1a ———▶	(cause) ———▶	2a
Control sample	1b ——————————————▶		2b

1a and 1b could be observations of identical empty gas jars. The intervention could be to fill one of these with damp beans. 2a and 2b are observations made after a few days have passed. Any differences observed at the end of the experiment can be attributed to the insertion of the beans. The confidence in this conclusion depends on the control exerted to ensure that all conditions were identical for experimental and control gas jar, apart from the insertion of the beans. Extraneous factors have been controlled. There are many variations on this basic design, but it is the model from which causes can be inferred and predictions made.

The problems of this design with humans as subjects start with the rarity with which random allocation is possible, outside the psychological laboratory. In education it is rare because teachers will not allow existing classes to be disturbed or redistributed to form experimental and control groups. To the disturbance is added the reluctance to confine the experiment to only some of the children. So researchers have to use existing classes in a quasi experiment, thus increasing the chance of extraneous factors intervening. Furthermore, in real life, control cannot be maintained for any length of time. Extraneous factors accumulate as the days go by. Thus the maturation of children in the experiment, or unanticipated external events can be influential. Where tests are used at start and finish progress can be boosted by familiarity. Children can drop out of either experimental or control groups. Frequently these educational experiments lack a control group. This 'before and after' design is very common in assessing the impact of a new teaching method or curriculum. But as there is no control, there can be no certainty that extraneous factors have not caused any differences that occur. Thus no conclusions are possible as external and often unappreciated events could have influenced the results, including the enthusiasm of the teachers involved for the innovation.

The quasi experiment has been illustrated in Controversy 8. Typically it has left this debate over the pros and cons of mixed ability grouping wide open. It has shown how much more complicated the issue is than conceived by early protagonists and researchers. In particular the large-scale Barker Lunn study showed the key role of teachers' attitudes in determining the success of the grouping chosen.[1] It may be disappointing that experiments tend to be inconclusive. But this drives home the message that it is unlikely that any single innovation is ever going to have dramatic results in an activity so complex as education. The control exercised enables some of the intervening factors to be identified. But no experiment with humans can identify all the factors involved. Even where they can be identified there can often be only crude indicators to observe or measure.

This balance sheet of quasi experimentation can be illustrated from evaluations in education as elsewhere. It is rare for any large-scale, well-designed evaluation to conclude strongly for or against an innovation. Burstall's *French in the Primary School* is an exception in being conclusively against, but only because the innovation had little apparent effect.[2] Most evaluations are doomed to inconclusiveness by the nature of the innovation and the way evaluators get involved. Typical are the evaluations of the Educational Priority Area (E.P.A.) schemes following the Plowden Report on *Children and their Primary Schools* in 1967.[3] First, there were no clear specifications in the report or in the brief for the evaluations about objectives or procedures. Many of the projects spread small resources over large numbers of schools, making it unlikely that there would be any detectable payoff. Second, the evaluators were often late on the scene, unable to design their work before the project was under way. No control groups could be formed. Third, it is unlikely that even very well-funded innovations are going to have much impact given the inertia in a large enterprise such as education. The author was once asked to evaluate the impact of £10,000 allocated to the teaching of Asian languages in London's schools as part of the Inner City Partnership schemes. If you put peanuts in, you get peanuts out. This project promised a few hundred pounds for each language. Evaluation would have been a farce.

Controversy 4 also illustrates the problems with *ex post facto* experimentation. It seems a straightforward task to collect the examination results of comprehensive schools and to compare these with the combined results of grammar and secondary modern schools. The Controversy shows how difficult it is to control factors when reconstructing an experiment. There always seem to be factors not under control or not even anticipated that could have caused the differences detected. Similarly, Controversy 7 shows that reconstruction of events for *ex post facto* experimentation gets more difficult as time goes by. Historical studies are *ex post facto* and there is no chance of controlling the factors of interest and not even the certainty that the really important factors have been recovered. Palaeontologists have the hardest time of all. Just as they produce a theory from their scattered fossil evidence, somebody digs up another set of bones that shows how wrong they were.

Correlational research has become popular with computers which enable researchers to examine the relationship between large numbers of variables involved in such a process as teaching or learning. The difficulties are outlined in Controversy 2. But relationships are not causes. The variables manipulated may not add up to the complex process of schooling. Rutter's use of the term 'ethos' is an attempt to give some meaning to a mass of process variables.[4] But the relation may have only been statistical. Schools may have a detectable ethos, but it is not the sum total of a number of discrete process factors.

Experimental and experimenter effects

There are two closely related features of experiments involving humans that produce powerful extraneous factors that can become more important in influencing results than the innovation under investigation. Experimental effects arise from responses to being involved in an experiment. Experimenter effects arise from the influence of the researcher on the subjects. Both illustrate the problems of research into human behaviour. The respondents aren't passive. They interact with each other and the researcher, interpret what is going on and respond accordingly.

The effect of being involved in an experiment was first observed in the studies of the Hawthorne works of the General Electric Company in Chicago between 1924 and 1927.[5] These studies, intially concerned with productivity, were organised by Mayo at the Harvard Graduate School of Business and have been responsible for a shift in emphasis within industrial psychology. They have also provided the foundations for the human relations school of management. The reason for the lasting influence of these studies despite criticisms of their design will be discussed later.[6] Their importance here is the detection of the impact of being involved in an experiment on the workers in the factory. After experimental manipulation of the material conditions of work it was concluded that productivity depended primarily on the human relations involved and that the interest shown in the workers by the experimenters was the main factor behind their extra efforts. Indeed, even the deliberate worsening of material conditions of work seemed to have resulted in extra production due to the worker's feeling of being of concern to someone in authority. While these assumptions have been challenged on political as well as methodological grounds, the actual impact on the subjects of experimentation has been repeatedly confirmed.

This is often referred to as Hawthorne, or experimental effect. People under observation do not behave normally, but respond to the experimental conditions. The Hawthorne workers responded in a way that defeated the original purpose of the experiment and initiated a series of further investigations into the human relations that were influencing productivity and turnover of labour. An extraneous variable, initially unrecognised and therefore un-controlled, had intervened and in many cases proved more influential than the variable of physical environment originally being manipulated. Experiments on humans are always subject to this effect which, if not controlled, may bias results.

In the ideal experiment there are simply subject and stimulus under the control of, but not influenced by, an experimenter. But in experiments with humans, interaction is inevitable. The researcher cannot remain neutral however hard he tries to standardise his actions. He greets the subjects, settles them down, varies his words, gestures and expressions, just as they vary theirs. The experimenter steps out of his role to become interested in a pretty girl, to put a shy person at ease, to stop a child crying or comfort an old lady. In doing so he is breaching his controls over himself and making himself a factor in the experiment. He is giving clues to his subjects through which they can interpret the situation and get an idea how to respond.

Rosenthal, in his book *Experimenter Effects in Behavioural Research*,[7] provides plentiful evidence of such extraneous variables, including his own experiments devised to test the effect on results of the expectations of the experimenter. In this work there is no indication of how these expectations were communicated to the subjects, but the process may be similar to that described previously where the owners of clever animals or mind readers managed to convey the requisite answer. If this is the case it is particularly relevant for experiments in education, for children in school are prepared to look for clues about correct answers.

The history of education is strewn with simple solutions to complicated problems. But it is unlikely that a panacea for a many-sided symptom such as low attainment in school will suddenly be discovered. It is far more likely that the steady accumulation of evidence on the effectiveness of different methods of teaching, or approaches to individual children will affect improvement, than the discovery of a more potent style overnight. There is a lot of evidence to suggest that the self-image of a child is an important factor in determining achievement. But the nature of that image, the psychological and environmental factors that affect it, and the limits within which it can determine attainments are only slowly being uncovered. Yet in 1968, Rosenthal and Jacobson published *Pygmalion in the Classroom*,[8] describing an experiment in which teacher's expectations of children's performance were shown to bring that performance up to the expectations.

Rosenthal was a social psychologist who had an established reputation for his work on experimenter effects. This work at Harvard established a new field for psychological research. Jacobson was a school administrator. The book was hailed as a revelation in the popular press.[9] It remains one of the most widely quoted books on education, and Pygmalion effects became the basis of much pedagogical work in teacher training. But the psychologists who reviewed the book were mainly critical.[10] It seemed out-of-line with other work and the experimental design looked sloppy. Once

Rosenthal and Jacobson had provided their data for reanalysis, and their methods were scrutinised, a thorough demolition was published, confirming the doubts of earlier reviewers.[11] Work on the effects of expectations continues, but this episode on *Pygmalion in the Classroom* is a reason for caution and scepticism.

The reviews of *Pygmalion in the Classroom* by psychologists focused on reliability. In particular Thorndike pointed out that the gains only applied to nineteen of the children and that for the rest gains were small, or that there was a deterioration following higher expectations.[12] Indeed, more children deteriorated than gained. But Thorndike, like other reviewers, was most concerned with the test used and the way results were analysed. To him, the data were so untrustworthy that any conclusions had to be suspect. Other reviewers pointed out that the teachers involved did not seem to have taken the experiment very seriously.[13] They may not have bothered to play their Pygmalion role. In natural experiments and intervention programmes it is assumed that the programme has been implemented. But later evaluations are often of the impact of resources applied for other than the intended purposes, or new methods that were never actually implemented.

The value of the Rosenthal and Jacobson study as a controversy comes from their release of their data to other researchers. Under the auspices of the National Society for the Study of Education, Elashoff and Snow published *Pygmalion Reconsidered* in 1971.[14] This reanalysis of the data, brings together reviews and other related work and contains a defence by Rosenthal and Jacobson. But the conclusions of Elashoff and Snow are an indictment. Text and tables were seen as inconsistent, conclusions were over-dramatised, variables were misleadingly labelled and the findings were over-generalised.

The reviews of related work show that nine direct attempts to replicate Rosenthal and Jacobson's work failed.[15] The remaining work suggests that there is a relation between expectations and performance, but it is limited in scope and requires more than superficial attempts to modify the way teachers treat children. The work continues, but in spite of *Pygmalion in the Classroom*, rather than being boosted by it. Indeed, public confidence in psychological research could have been undermined by this episode, and the beneficial effects of getting teachers to raise their expectations of children thrown out with the discredited book. But few read the *American Educational Research Journal* or other professional publications where the criticisms were voiced, and Rosenthal and Jacobson's work remains on the menu in teacher education and in the folklore of teaching.

In the social sciences the most usual experiment takes the present situation as the effect of some past event and then traces back to establish a relation between the two. But the degree of control over the many variables involved tends to be small. It would be interesting to trace the education of successful people to see if factors such as attending public or progressive schools were important. But education is not definable as a single factor and many other influences will have been at work. It may be possible to match groups to eliminate the effect of some of these extraneous factors, but reliability is likely to be low and alternative explanations for the present situation being investigated cannot be eliminated. History, politics, economics and sociology abound with the resulting controversies between rival schools of thought, all claiming support from analysis after the event.

The major obstacle in any *ex post facto* explanation is that the causes indicated could never have been used to predict the event. Everyone theorises about the causes of crime or war by examining past events, but none of the combinations of actions suggested as the cause exhausts all the possible combinations. These explanations are plausible only because the event has already occurred. Such experiments are always inadequate. Different people will choose different factors and give each factor a different weight in the explanation.

CONTROVERSY 8

WHEN WAS CHILDHOOD DISCOVERED?

It may seem odd that there is a dispute about the point in history when childhood was recognised as a distinct stage in human development. But childhood is an abstraction and historians and social scientists debate how models of childhood have been constituted in contrasting cultures at different times. The publication of Ariès's *Centuries of Childhood* in 1962 was particularly important, for here childhood was seen as an invention of the last 300 years.[1] Was there then no concept of childhood before the seventeenth century? Is caring mothering a modern development?

The first step to an answer to this question lies not in data from research but, as usual, in the theoretical models employed. There is great variety. Each theory leads to a different view of children and each leads to different emphases in research and evidence. In the nineteenth and early twentieth century childhood was seen as biologically determined. Psychologists such as Piaget saw children as moving in stages towards adulthood and the norms of mature behaviour.[2] That progress is measured against adult yardsticks and hence is often described as a series of stages of development. Some sociologists such as Parsons have taken a similar view, seeing child socialisation as the process through which adult norms and roles are learned.[3] But other sociologists see childhood as a construction. Here the child is not defined by its progress towards adult behaviour, towards a part in the social system, or 'what is to be', but through looking at the interactions of children and adults to see how childhood is defined in the present. Here childhood is defined by interacting interpretations not external, concrete norms.

This distinction between theories that define childhood against adult norms or as biologically determined, and those that see it as constituted through interaction is crucial in understanding how a debate over the existence of childhood could occur. If childhood is defined differently in different cultures at different times there is room for disagreement and examples can be found to support any view however extreme. Only if some biological unfolding or progress towards some unchanging adult role is assumed should there be surprise at conflicting views on the existence of childhood and its content.

Ariès's *Centuries of Childhood* became holy writ in the 1960s. Through his studies of French children he concluded that medieval society throughout Europe did not recognise childhood. The evidence produced suggested that children were viewed as inseparable from adults. They were painted as small adults, dressed like them and were treated without consideration of their physical, mental or sexual immaturity. Aries was not arguing that children were necessarily neglected or ill-treated, but that mothers were indifferent because the awareness of children as fully human was missing. As soon as the infant could survive without the constant attention of mother or nurse, he or she joined adult society. The infants who were too fragile to participate in adult life were not taken into account. If they died, that was God's will.

Ariès's thesis received support from many other authors maintaining that childhood was a product of modernisation.[4] Some went as far as claiming that before modern times children were not even seen as human. Childhood came to be accepted as invented about 300 years ago. To Aries this invention produced the restrictions on the behaviour of children in the modern family. When children were not seen as separate from adults they were given licence to behave as adults. Identification as children led to an often strict upbringing to ensure that they were morally and physically chaste. To Sommerville this increased attention to children was due to competition between the churches following the Reformation.[5] Child rearing was brought into line with Christian thought. Children were discovered through religious competiton.

Ariès's work rests on an analysis of images of children in historical sources. Twenty years after the publication of *Centuries of Childhood* his thesis has been challenged. Pollock maintains that there were very few changes in the care given to children from the sixteenth to the nineteenth century and that parents have always seemed to have enjoyed their offspring.[6] But while the criticisms of Ariès have proliferated, there is disagreement among the critics. Thus, De Mause challenges Ariès's thesis that the laxity of children's lives was replaced by severe restriction and punishment in modern times.[7] He lists page after page of horrifying detail of children being 'killed, abandoned, beaten, terrorised and sexually abused' in the ancient world. If the invention of childhood led to more pain than this it would indeed be incredible. The history of childhood to De Mause is a nightmare only ending with modernisation.

This controversy revolves around historical documents. How then could an historian such as Ariès come to conclusions that seem absurd only a decade after the publication of a book seen as definitive?

The answer lies in the documents used, their interpretation and the model of childhood built into the thesis. Ariès depended heavily for his ideas that childhood is a modern invention on paintings. Yet it seems odd to assume that medieval artists could only depict a child as a little adult. Changes would have been the result of changing conventions in art as much as changing views on those painted. Wilson in an appraisal of Ariès concludes that the artistic representation of children was changed as artists in the Renaissance discovered Greek and Roman art.[8] Artistic convention rather than knowledge of children was the basis for the little adults.

The use of documents on how to rear children is also suspect. Fortunately, given its frequent lunacy, expert advice to parents is usually ignored. That applies as much as to a twentieth century psychologist such as Watson, the 'father of American psychology', who warned mothers against hugging or kissing their children in the 1920s, as to divines, moralists and quacks in earlier times.[9] Most mothers follow their parents or learn from neighbours.

The problem with the evidence used by Ariès is that it is secondary. It is his interpretation of interpretations by doctors, or artists, or preachers. Since the publication of Ariès's book Ladurie's reconstruction of life in fourteenth-century Montaillou has been published.[10] This is based on the answers of the peasants themselves when questioned by the Inquisition. Ladurie concludes from his primary sources that parental attitudes were similar to ours

600 years later. Women grieved for their dead children, loved them and were not afraid to express these feelings. They were certainly not indifferent.

If the reliability and validity of the historical documents used by Ariès are suspect, there is more trouble with his focus on the rich and the royals, particularly the young Louis XIII. Royal families are not typical and there seems to have been a lot of hanky panky in the Louvre at the time. The majority of the people do not leave written records. But when Pollock reviewed a wide range of sources, a more humane and human picture emerges.[11] It is still largely a world of the literate, the propertied and male. But to Pollock the bulk of historians of childhood have been incorrect. They deal with a minority only and have misinterpreted the evidence. There has been too much 'exampling', collecting evidence to support a thesis while ignoring that which could refute it.

The temptation to select data to support a thesis leads back to Chapter 1 and the debate over the nature of science. The data collected and their interpretation into evidence is directed by theoretical models of the topic studied, often shared by a 'scientific community'. Students of childhood start with implicit or explicit models. Most of these seem to assume a passive child.

It seems odd that while the social sciences have changed dramatically across this century and while they conflict in their views of human behaviour and organisation, they share a view of childhood that is usually deterministic. Children are seen as funnelled by genes, or the unfolding of history, or social controls, towards pre-determined adult behaviour. To Mount this is the result of persisting Victorian beliefs in evolution, in stages of development from lower to higher.[12] Like Pollock, Mount sees continuity in child care across the ages once the researcher gets to the primary sources and stops gathering examples to fit pre-specified stages of development. In most theoretical models, as with many religious or moralistic views of children, the child is led to some existing adult world. But children are not just the subject of biological, psychological or cultural pressures. They use culture, they interpret the messages from adults and from teachers and media. Indeed, any parent can confirm that children convert men and women into fathers and mothers.[13] Children are active in their own socialisation and the older they get in societies where dependence is extended to and through higher education, the more their interpretations count. The model used influences the evidence presented. The bulk of the available evidence is modelled as a child being pressed towards some pre-determined adult role. A different model, giving more emphasis to activity initiated by the child would produce different evidence.

8

DOCUMENTS, UNOBTRUSIVE MEASURES AND TRIANGULATION

Going to the literature is the start of all research, as it is to writing essays or revising for examinations. In this search the four questions which started this book should be asked. The way the information is extracted and used, its validity and the representativenesss of the source should always be questioned. So should the availability of enough detail on how the evidence was collected to enable reliability and validity to be assessed. Controversy 7 illustrated this danger in using paintings, books, diaries and tracts in reconstructing the history of childhood. The controversy exists because researchers tend to select evidence that supports their views. In this chapter the focus is on the way documents are used by professional researchers. But the cautions apply to all enquiry that refers to documents, statistics and indicators of human behaviour.

Conflicting views on children illustrate the way theoretical models determine the way data are converted into evidence and hence documents. If children are seen as little angels, their misdemeanours are blamed on the social conditions or on problem parents. If they are seen as little devils their peccadillos are seen and recorded as the workings of Satan, original sin or unfortunate genes. If you don't know the model used by the author you have to guess at the interpretation. When documents are used there is an additional problem. The author has already carried out a prior interpretation of the source used. Indeed, most books are interpretations of interpretations of interpretations and so on.

Most books are not based on information gathered for the purpose but are collections of material, often first published in articles, that have been organised by the author to present a new perspective on an issue. Thus articles usually rest on primary sources of data, books on secondary sources and later books on tertiary material from earlier ones. At each step, distance from the original study lends a misleading enchantment to the reliability of the primary source. The original article may have a cautious section on methods, the first book briefly mentions them and later ones just quote the evidence, not how it was obtained. Thus tentative suggestions may become hard facts.

This tendency for doubts about reliability to diminish with the distance from the original also applies to the extraction of evidence from documents. All documents are distant from the reality they may reflect. The Census deals with the basic statistics of the population at a given date. But the data are given by a citizen, tabulated by another and interpreted by the reader. Mistakes can happen. Juvenile persons frequent some areas and pensioners some schools. When the document is an account which contains interpretations, the distance from reality can be further barricaded by slanted perceptions. *Mein Kampf* would not be studied as a dependable historical document, but it was only one stage removed from the conditions that Hitler was observing. Other documents are secondary in being written by an author after interpreting other documents. There can be a long chain of such interpretations. At each stage the chance of bias increases.

The distance between document and reality, and the number of interpretations involved have to be considered in interpreting documentary evidence. Even research reports have to be interpreted with caution. A local education authority may want information on the state of its schools. It instructs its inspectors and advisers to collect the data. The collected information is sorted through by a senior inspector and a selection of reports summarised. The report then goes in draft to colleagues. Informal consultations take place with political members. Suggestions are received and revisions made. A draft goes to education committee and after amendments, a version is made public. Even before the document becomes available it may have become an instrument for change, a support for policies, a reflection of professional opinion rather than an image of reality. All documents go through similar stages. This is no different from the sequence of interpretations that link the start of an idea for research, through the collection of data, to the preparation and publication of a report.

In sociology, the user of documents has also to take notice of the phenomenological view outlined in Chapter 3. The police, the courts, doctors, teachers and so on produce reports which at every stage of processing identify and confirm people as delinquents, or sick or under-attaining. Individuals are slotted into categories. The coding of data for processing by computer is a typical categorising procedure, often involving mutilation to obtain a fit. Documents are problematic. To Cicourel each report must be treated as a particular interpretation within a particular situation. His book, *The Social Organization of Juvenile Justice*,[1] uses records, but not as a source of information on delinquents, but to show how they come to be defined as delinquent. With this view, even the report full of statistical tables must be seen as a particular way of categorising, not as some immutable, consistent and agreed formulation. The assessment of evidence derived from documents requires the same basic questions to be answered as with all forms of research. The test of reliability is still whether another researcher would extract the same information from the available documents. There is still a need to assess whether enough care has been taken to ensure that superfluous information has not been taken as central. Finally the extent to which the information that has been extracted can be generalised has to be determined. Reliability and validity are still central issues.

Historical documents

We can now return to the study of Polish peasants by Thomas and Znaniecki.[2] Not only is this a classic study using the analysis of documents but it has also been subjected to a thorough retrospective evaluation. The authors were concerned with the problems of social change and particularly of immigration. They adopted the viewpoint that such a study, as in all sociology, was necessarily concerned with the way individuals interpreted the situations they were in as well as with the circumstances themselves. Because there was this emphasis on the importance of subjective factors, personal documents were selected as the source of materials for analysis. These were assumed to reveal individual attitudes to events.

The documents used included letters, autobiographies, newspapers, court records and records of social agencies.[3] There was no clear account in the book of the way these materials were obtained. The letters seem to have been bought after an advertisement had been placed in a Polish émigré journal published in North America. The newspapers were bought in Poland by Thomas while on a visit. His search for documentary evidence on Polish life involved adventures connected with the outbreak of the First World War that were not only unanticipated, but resulted in much material being left in a central European hotel by a courier fleeing from the authorities to avoid being called up for the army. Again none of this farce appeared in the final books where the actual method of collecting the data was largely ignored.

Documents were collected from an agency concerned with emigration from Poland. There were records from émigré Polish societies in America and court records from areas around Chicago with large Polish populations. Finally there was a long autobiography by a Pole who had only recently left his native land. Blumer, assessing the reliability of these documents as sources from which a picture of changing society could be drawn, concluded that they were inadequate.[4] They were fragmentary, discontinuous, leaving gaps that had to be filled in through the knowledge and imagination of the authors. The letters which formed the bulk of the documentary evidence gave no picture of the background or living conditions of the writers. The picture presented in the book was drawn by the authors, interpreting the material and filling in the gaps from their own knowledge of Polish life. Thomas himself admitted that he and Znaniecki were 'indisputably in the wrong' to give the impression that the theories in the book were founded on data.

Arising out of the Social Science Research Council's conference in 1938 to discuss *The Polish Peasant*, four studies of the use of personal documents were commissioned, one each for sociology, psychology, history and anthropology. Gottschalk, reviewing the use of documents in history selects as the first problem for the historian the establishment of the authenticity of the document.[5] Second, if the document is reliable, the credibility of the evidence in it has to be determined. The historian adopts the attitude of the lawyer towards evidence, questioning the ultimate source of the evidence, the ability and honesty of the witness and the accuracy with which he has been reported in the document. Finally he looks for corroboration by independent sources. Third, the historian has to assess the relevance of the information. It is useful historically only if it relates to other history rather than standing as an isolated incident, however interesting.

Thus Gottschalk is asking whether the text is genuine, and if so, what is it really saying. However, while all users of documents should be concerned with their reliability and validity, the historian has his own conceptual framework and methods of investigation that alert him to the need for caution. The historian is trained to reconstruct past events by reference to their specific place and time. The historian's use of documents is grounded within this context. Social scientists, concerned more with change than with concrete events, use documents more freely. But the absence of reference to a particular time and place and the absence of training in using documents in the social sciences often results in uncritical use. Historians spend lifetimes in establishing the authenticity of documents. Others seize them without thought as convenient grist to their mill.

In a fifth study commissioned from Dollard, the criteria for assessing life histories were examined.[6] Of particular importance is Dollard's views on the way sense is made of material and of the way it is pieced together until it has meaning. Here the way social scientists use their models to make sense of data is stressed in order to alert the reader to it as a problem in assessing credibility. Those life histories that have been examined tend to come out rather well. For example, Clifford Shaw's 'jack roller' or mugger was re-interviewed fifty years after the original study and it was confirmed that the relationship had been deep and long-lasting.[7]

There is however another question about representativeness in life histories. There is no doubt that social scientists, like journalists, are attracted by the eccentric and no doubt their respondents stressed their successes or spectacular failures rather than the boring parts of their lives. By the time the account has been written by the researchers, the subjects appear as suspiciously articulate. Thus Sutherland's *Professional Thief* suggests a man of unusual talent.[8] Snodgrass, diligently tracing Chic Conwell into the 1940s, even though he was supposed to have died in 1933, has drawn a picture of a very charming, articulate, entertaining and shrewd man very capable of writing accounts of his crimes for Sutherland, the most eminent criminologist of his day.[9] He was also very clear about the way Sutherland had taken over and interpreted his writings.

The use of life histories seems to be having a revival.[10] Goodson has traced changes in school subjects by collecting together histories of important innovators.[11] By relating the interviews to curriculum histories, Goodson locates curriculum change in its historical context. He admits that the picture is partial, may lack authenticity and may have been contributed by unrepresentative figures. But it does correct the assumption behind much research that people interpret their situations, give them meaning and create their own reality, as if the past never existed.

Statistics as constructions of reality

The difficulty in interpreting statistics can be seen in an area where they abound.[12] There are annual statistics of crime from the Commissioners of Prisons, the Council for Central After-Care, the Commissioner of Police for the Metropolis, the Home Office Research Unit, from criminologists and above all the *Criminal Statistics for England and Wales*. Yet these apparent riches cannot even confirm that crime is increasing or decreasing.

The first problem is that the statistics cannot include crimes committed but not reported, or not considered by the police to fit the categories used. An apparent crime wave can result from the public being convinced that they should now report some category of crime such as rape, or from the police becoming more concerned or more efficient in dealing with it. Similarly, some crimes go out of fashion as the public reports them less often or the police switch attention elsewhere. Police practice rather than criminal activity can be paramount. They may concentrate on stopping mugging or prostitution, often following a campaign in the media. Putting the spotlight on a crime increases its incidence through extra police diligence. Elsewhere, other crimes may apparently decrease as police switch away from them. Criminals may also confess to more crimes than they committed once caught, particularly if the police are persuasive, thus apparently increasing the number cleared up.

The second set of problems is that there is no connection between the sets of statistics. One criminal may commit 100 crimes or 100 villains may commit one each. Try to interpret the relation between 292 blackmail cases in 1965 and the 179 persons prosecuted.[13] The third problem is that any statistics conceal messy reality. Overworked policemen and clerks fit individual cases into general categories. The public won't report crimes if they think the law unfair. Policemen take it easy on the streets because they depend on getting information from those on the edge of crime. Police concentrate resources where they seem to be most needed. This usually means concentrating in working-class areas or where business property has to be protected. The police do not usually concern themselves with fiddling of income tax and other white-collar crimes. They are also wary of excessive zeal in pursuing traffic offences which might jeopardise public relations. Within the police system, too, procedures are necessarily arbitrary and imprecise. The author, while station constable in the police, once refused to listen to a woman who complained four times in one week about being assaulted by her boyfriend. The fifth time she encountered a more sympathetic ear and action was taken which resulted in a three-year prison sentence for the man concerned. It is on such chances that statistics are built.

The fourth problem is that official statistics do not necessarily reflect reality, but often construct it. This is extensively documented in *Demystifying Social Statistics*.[14] Here statistics are shown to be creations, not stored-up facts. They are constructed not produced. Furthermore, that construction is not directed by a neutral state machinery, but one with a distinctive capitalist ideology that affects definitions and procedures. Once again evidence is seen to be the product of the framework of ideas, theories and models within which the methods for its collection are designed. Political as well as academic and personal views play their part.

Unobtrusive measures and triangulation

The advantage of documents as sources of evidence is that they have been compiled for other purposes than to provide information for social scientists or historians. They can be assumed to be a reflection of feelings undisturbed by the presence of the researcher. This is also the case with other traces of activity. Humans leave evidence of their activities around, and alert social scientists can use this source to build up a picture of natural behaviour. Webb and others have produced a book on such sources.[15] They range from counting the liquor bottles in dustbins to measuring the wear on carpets in museums.

Few of these measures are sufficient by themselves to provide reliable data. But they are an important confirmatory source unaffected by the researcher. They can add both insight into and actual measures of human behaviour. Their limitations are those already suggested for all documents, plus the often unsystematic way in which the evidence has accumulated or has to be collected. Nevertheless such measures are probably an important and neglected source of evidence, avoiding many of the snags associated with research involving obtrusion into human activity.

In practice, unobtrusive measures probably play an important if accidental part in most research. The social scientist going about his everyday activities is alerted to the behaviour of others by the discipline he practises. As he drinks his beer in the pub, squeezes into the tube train or sits in the cinema he takes in the scene with an eye skilled in fitting casual observations into the orderly model in his mind. As he gets involved in planning a research project these models are sensitive to relevant perceptions so that his hunches emerge from a combination of theorising and casual observation.

The most frequently used unobtrustive measures are documents. The writers usually produce them unaware that a social researcher is lurking in the present or will be probing in the future. The Polish Peasant studies were based on letters. These first came to the attention of Thomas when some were thrown at his feet out of a window in a pile of garbage.[16] It pays to be alert to the serendipitous if unobtrusive measures are prized for their validity.

The technical term for the use of two or more methods of collecting data is triangulation.[17] When research is reported it often appears as if only one method has been used. In practice experiments are backed by observations, ethnography includes interviews and many researchers committed to observation produce questionnaires to give them another source of information.

All back their work with documentary evidence. Furthermore, many techniques for gathering data 'triangulate' by using historical or comparative information to add time and space dimensions. There can also be analysis at the individual as well as the collective level, employing psychological as well as sociological insights. Contrasting or conflicting theories can be employed presenting the reader with alternative explanations.

A good example of triangulation is the study of 'Bishop McGregor' school by Burgess.[18] Here ethnography is supplemented by analyses of letters and documents available in the school and from autobiographies and diaries prepared by the teachers. Burgess provided the framework for these and teachers gave him two pages of personal detail and diaries covering one month of teaching 'Newsom' children. These were followed up by 'diary interviews'. Behind this cooperation lies a host of investment in synchronising the methods and building-up the necessary rapport.

Triangulation is an appropriate idea at which to close this part on methods. Throughout, the reader has been recommended to look for flaws in reliability. The most vulnerable research is the single investigator using one method on a politically sensitive issue. Investigator triangulation, the technical term for having at least two researchers, at least reduces the chance of intentional bias. Other forms of triangulation can compensate for the unreliability of a single method. But the last point has to be key question four. Is there enough information for the research to be assessed in the published report? If there is not, the more personal and professional issues raised in Part 3 have to be given priority.

PART 3

THE PERSONAL AND POLITICAL INFLUENCES ON RESEARCH

The focus now shifts from the technical design of social research in Part 2 to the limitations imposed by personal, professional and political aspects. All science is context-bound. Pythagoras and Galileo were as affected by their times as Newton or Einstein by theirs. The impact is at the personal as well as the professional level. Scientists are human in seeking rewards and prestige. They hold political beliefs and strive to change the world. Science is bound by conventions, but these are punctured by external influences.

This context-bound view of science also follows from the analysis in Part 1. If science was the free-ranging, open-minded observation of the world, scientists could possibly remain insulated from social pressures, acting-out the eccentric, single and often absent-minded role that is the popular parody. But, bound into a community, directed towards soluble problems defined by shared theoretical positions, often working in large teams and dependent on money from government or corporation, today's scientist has limited scope for eccentricity. Prestige, promotion and publication depend on obtaining communal support. Science is expensive and the communities meet the demands of those with power and money. Nevertheless, personal and political pressures are influential.

While human science is cheaper, still open to the individual worker, and, with its youth, less bound into established research communities, it is even more open to external pressures. Its subject matter is itself personal and political. Here the division between research using controlled methods and including interpretive, ethnographic approaches, and investigation explicitly aimed to improve the human lot is important. Much research is on the poor, the disadvantaged, the deviant and the oppressed, or on the structures that maintain their disadvantage. Staying neutral is ethically dubious in such cases. What is important is not so much whether a human scientist takes sides, as whether his position is spelled out for the reader. That is why there was a fourth question about information made available in the introduction. We are now to be concerned with the assumptions and expectations of researchers and the way these define the scope and limitations of social research.

9

THE AUTHOR, THE DATE AND THE CONTEXT

Controversies 1 and 3 were both concerned with long-lasting debate over the part played by nature and nurture in forming human intelligence. It is difficult to appreciate either the span of years of this debate, its fury or its tragic political applications. Its origins are clear in the usually abbreviated title of Darwin's classic *On the Origin of Species by Means of Natural Selection or the Preservation of Favoured Races in the Struggle for Life*. Francis Galton, Darwin's half cousin, saw the Jews as 'specialised for a parasitic existence upon other nations . . . .'[1] The superiority of the white race came to be accepted. The development of intelligence testing confirmed this superiority. Immigrants into America, foreigners and blacks were shown to have lower scores than indigenous white populations. As long as the tests were seen to be culture-free this scientific support for racism persisted. Hitler's 'final solution' of the Jewish problem was only one horrific episode of inhumanity backed by this genetic science.

It took over fifty years for the criticisms of intelligence tests to be accepted and for their use in selection for secondary schooling to be reduced. They are still extensively used in psychology. During the fifty years up to his death in 1971 the dominant figure in British educational psychology was Cyril Burt. He played a major part in the development of standardised tests. It is now accepted that he invented evidence to support this case for the inheritance of intelligence.[2] The controversy is over the way in which he could do this and remain as an acknowledged leader of his profession, knighted in 1946 and showered with academic honours.

The authoritative source for an answer is Hearnshaw's biography. Hearnshaw delivered the address at the Memorial Service for Burt

1971 and was asked to write his biography by Burt's sister.[3] She provided a grant for the task and the dead man's accumulated papers. However, before Hearnshaw could start to write, Kamin published an attack on Burt in 1974, not only detailing carelessness in presenting data but evidence of fraud in statistical calculation.[4] In the *Sunday Times* of 24 October 1976 under the headline 'Crucial data was faked by eminent psychologist', Oliver Gillie, the *Times* medical correspondent, spelled out that Burt had falsified data, invented crucial facts, converted guesses into certainties, worked back from the results he wanted to make the observations fit and even invented the collaborators listed as co-authors in key articles.[5] Hearnshaw concludes that these charges were correct. Burt's later work was fraudulent.

Burt's main interests were individual differences and heredity. These aspects were dominated early in this century by the work of Francis Galton, himself directly influenced by Darwin. Burt was not only heavily influenced by Galton but met him as a near neighbour while a young man. Burt described his work as preserving and developing the Galtonian tradition. To Hearnshaw, Burt formulated his life's goals with clarity and assurance and stuck to them tenaciously through his long life. That tenacity was to include fraud.

There are two major anomalies in the story of Cyril Burt. First, there is no doubting the humanity as well as the integrity of his work for the disadvantaged while educational psychologist for the London County Council between 1913 and 1932. Burt believed that intelligence was innate. He first published this conclusion in 1909 based on research with a sample of forty three. To Hearnshaw these slender findings were seen by Burt as 'conclusive'. By the time of his death Burt saw them as 'incontestable'. His later years were devoted to consolidating this evidence. Yet he used his influence to get a better deal for 'backward' children, and much of the contemporary concern for special educational needs originates with Burt's work on individual differences.

The second anomaly is more embarrassing if less well documented. Burt was a dominant figure in educational psychology. He was also revered by his students and colleagues. Yet he was devious and unscrupulous in getting his own way. This extended to re-writing contributions to the *British Journal of Educational*

Psychology which he edited and to faking letters supporting his position to his other journal, the *British Journal of Statistical Psychology*. Yet the community of British psychologists remained silent in face of this dishonesty. The controversy broke after Burt's death in 1971. It was sparked off by work in America and the *Times* newspaper article. The only British contribution to the exposure was by Clarke and Clarke in 1974.[6]

It is easy to speculate on why Burt resorted to fraud. Hearnshaw sees Burt in old age as increasingly paranoic, continually fabricating evidence to support his views on the inheritance of intelligence as evidence accumulated particularly in sociology, to refute it.

At the heart of this controversy is not the deceit of an old man, but the failure of a scientific community. However august, however central the authority of a scientist like Burt within British psychology for fifty years from 1920 to 1970, there should still have been protest and exposure before his death. Scientists carry authority because they superseded seers and priests through the exercise of informed scepticism and systematic enquiry. Amid all the different interpretations of scientific activity that duty to criticise remains.

Yet it is easy to see how there could have been silence amid fraud. If science proceeds from theoretical models to enquiry, acceptance of these models in a community can lead to doctoring results. They are expected and therefore accepted uncritically. The scientific community is also organised to consolidate the position of the great and good. The control of qualification, promotion and publication by seniors ensures not only quality but the likely rejection of anything critical of established beliefs. Within sociology as it expanded after 1950 there were a series of revolts by the young that ensured that criticism was swingeing. Psychology seems to have developed an establishment too early in its development and this may have muted the young critics. Rewards went to those who played within the rules and the game was dominated by authorities such as Burt. It is a warning that now switches the focus of this book to the personal and political aspects of social research.

HOW COULD PSYCHOLOGY INCLUDE FRAUD? THE CASE OF SIR CYRIL BURT

Burt's decline into fraud can be seen as a failure of a scientific community to question the great as it does the novice. This case, and other examples in this chapter, are exceptional. But in Chapter 10 the many ways in which evidence can be doctored and boosted are outlined. Authors dress up their evidence to create the best impression. They do this within conventions that change with the times. Books and articles do not just date because the evidence they contain is superseded. The redundancy can occur because of the way subject matter is modelled.

Over long periods of time the redundancy in print is obvious. We no longer think it harmful to hug our children as did our grandparents and have largely given up the idea that children are born evil. But very recent changes have also made yesterday's evidence look silly. The sociology of the 1960s was largely functionalist, based on an organic model of human society. Those of us who worked through that time may have been aware of the limitations of that model. We were less aware, if at all, that we had assumed a male world.

The invisibility of women in social research and in education has now been vigorously documented. It can be flavoured in the titles *Doing Feminist Research*[1] or *Breaking Out: Feminist Consciousness and Feminist Research*[2] or *Invisible Women*.[3] This was not just a tendency to use masculine terms. Models of social mobility, of educational opportunity, of the curriculum, of employment, largely ignored women. Today the activities of feminist researchers have exposed this male domination. A look at the literature of the 1960s such as Dale's *Mixed or Single-Sex School*[4] or Douglas's *The Home and the School*[5] show a world where girls were largely ignored. In less than twenty years there has been a radical switch in the focus of social research. Now it gives women a place on the stage. Even more important, women have begun to research into the sexist structure of society. Similar shifts have come in race, age and special need as bases of perception. But the caution is not just about the dating of evidence although this will continue. Today's literature still contains examples of white, Anglo-Saxon, Protestant, middle-aged, male and propertied perspectives. But so will tomorrow's. All that is certain is that we do not know today what bias will be detected in our work by our successors.

Authors have a variety of motives for writing. They have in common only a desire to spread information, exert influence and gain material rewards or prestige. The first major distinction is between books and articles that are attempts to produce reliable evidence and those that reflect only the views of the author. The presence of references to research results is no guarantee of objectivity. Flat-earthers have no difficulty accumulating convincing evidence. Lunatic theories of human behaviour are even easier to support by dependable-looking evidence.

A further distinction has to be made between books and articles in popular journals such as *New Society* or *Forum* and research papers published in journals for professionals such as the *British Journal of Psychology* or *Sociology*. Not only does the technical level of these articles differ, but so do the motives of the authors. Books and popular articles tend to be written as collections of work that has already appeared in professional journals. The writer of a book is paid by the publisher. In the social, as in the natural sciences, prestige is as likely to be lost as much as gained through the effort at reaching a wide audience. Whereas a research paper for fellow professionals is designed to advance existing knowledge about events or techniques, and must include sufficient description of methods to enable the readers to assess its reliability, a book or popular article tends to include only enough method to indicate how the information was obtained. Finally, fellow professionals are assumed to have read the literature relevant to the subject and all that is required is the shorthand of a few references. But a book or more popular article has to summarise and simplify this background material.

A most alarming development is the proliferation of 'readers' presenting extracts from a number of sources on a subject. Another is the production of simple, filleted versions for students. These present the core of the original without any accompanying description of methods and their shortcomings which appear in the original. No opportunity or invitation is given to assess reliability or validity. Students and public fed on a diet of readers and popular accounts would have little idea of the real nature of social science.

The real world of the social researcher

The assessment of social research requires a realistic image of the researcher. Because he is interested in social relationships he is liable to have strong views about them. The motive for research is often to promote change. For example, Lacey, starting out on his research later published as 'Hightown Grammar', reports receiving contradictory advice.[6] One set of colleagues advised a conventional detached view of schooling, but another group advised him to set about taking the lid off the grammar schools. Few social scientists now claim to be value-free. In practice scientists strive in directions and within limits established by the communities within which they work. The true and the valuable are not absolute standards, but are related to current scientific belief and practice. Natural science is not value-free, but permeated with values that each scientist learns as he becomes a fully accepted practitioner, as well as with personal opinions.

To Gouldner, the idea of value-free sociology is a group myth, a caste mark of the decorous.[7] It enables sociologists to be morally indifferent, to escape responsibility for the implications of their work and to escape from the world into academic security. To Mills it has enabled abstracted empiricism to dominate research activity so that sociologists can become fact-gatherers for administrators and can ignore important political issues.[8]

The consequences of the persistence of the value-free myth can be seen first in the wasteful proliferation of elaborate analyses of dubious data from questionnaires churned out by computers, which, as Runciman has pointed out, have produced nothing comparable in importance to the insights of classical social theorists.[9] These empirical studies supporting the ceilings of archive rooms in university libraries are often studies of the attitudes of students, the applications of new statistical techniques and comparisons of unlikely subjects such as primary education in Pimlico and eastern Tasmania. Each has contributed little to the sum of knowledge or the truth, but has qualified its author for membership of his community of peers by showing that he has learned the necessary procedures of research and reporting.

The second impact of values comes in the selection and survival of evidence until it virtually becomes part of the mythology of a subject. The Hawthorne studies have wide currency in the social sciences and subjects using such evidence.[10] But the original work has been strongly criticised. First, the conclusions on the superiority of good human relations over material conditions and monetary rewards do not seem related to the evidence produced. Second, the frailty of the evidence does not seem to justify the survival of the conclusions. The Hawthorne studies and the human relations movement they initiated were supports for, and were supported by, the prevailing climate of capitalism and democracy. Workers could be kept contented by democratic means.

A similar case is the Lewin, Lippitt and White experiments on different teaching climates.[11] Here the frequently reported results again support democratic leadership. But one of the original research workers has explained how he and his fellow students put their all into the democratic but not into the authoritarian or *laissez-faire* role.[12] They were experimenting while Hitler was still a menace.

The frequency with which both these experiments appear in textbooks can be explained by the support they give to paramount values in our culture. Both studies were an outstanding contribution to the development of social science. They are more reliable than most. Their fragility is unfortunate, but the selective nature of their survival is even more disturbing.

The researcher also faces problems in organising and publishing his work. It has to be financed. Access has to be obtained from organisations. Individuals have to be persuaded to cooperate. Government departments, advisers, inspectors and sponsoring bodies have to be satisfied that the work is worthwhile and the researcher trustworthy. Personal relations in research teams have to be kept amicable. Platt has listed ten points where practical, personal and organisation problems can affect work.[13] There are now accounts of the trials and tribulations of researchers. Platt's work was based on interviews with social scientists. Bell and Newby,[14] Shipman[15] and Burgess[16] have edited accounts of the experiences of researchers as they went about their work.

The picture that emerges from books on the process of social research is of enthusiasm, hard work, ingenuity, and perhaps a touch of acrimony. Dale describes the research load as involving two days' work in one.[17] He reports crises and periods of doubt, but twenty-six years of work around his subject have still left a thirst to find out more. John and Elizabeth Newson show how the birth of their own child focused their attention on child-rearing.[18] Later their punched cards, schedules and letters stack up in their living room. They describe this early work as a cottage industry. Bell reports on disagreements within the team studying Banbury and on unforeseen difficulties leading to delays in publication.[19] Ford looks back at her earlier research and sees someone floating a counter-rumour because of her disgust and fright at the replacement of one form of overt injustice within education by another more subtle and tenacious.[20] All through these accounts there are signs of strain, over-work overcome by enthusiasm. Douglas finds the weight of data in longitudinal studies creating the need for painful decisions to be made in order to get the evidence published.[21] After twenty-eight years with the study he remains convinced of its importance. The Newsons have to choose between the many demands on their services as their work produces more and more evidence. These researchers paint a personal picture of research as a human activity. Perhaps the image for the reader is of Dale, seriously ill for six months, trying to catch up in the face of assistants who administered tests wrongly, or tests that failed to arrive from the printers, a typing bar falling off the computer output, of programming problems and of mounting piles of data. Dale gives a picture of immersion in the work, 'during walks, driving the car, in bed at night, over the endless cups of tea in the study ...'.[22] Preoccupied in this way he nearly falls under the hooves of four cart horses pulling a brewer's dray.

The researcher's problems do not end when the evidence has been produced. It still has to be published. As Becker has pointed out, there is an irreducible conflict between the view of the researcher and those he studies.[23] Research is deflating, generalising and abstracting. Someone is going to feel insulted, even if others will feel comforted. Most researchers have experienced the twinges of conscience as they write critically about those who have allowed them access, answered their questions and taken them into their confidence. Problems can also arise within research teams over what should be published. Every researcher writes in the context of such minor or major dilemmas. These are not as dramatic as the publication of the Pentagon papers, but the reader should recognise that researchers usually face tough decisions. They do not want to appear parasitic, biters of the hands that fed them coffee, nor to queer the pitch for those that follow. Yet they feel obliged to report honestly, and there is mileage in revelation.

The date of publication

There is always a possibility of redundancy in books and articles. This springs partly from the lapse of time between completing research and getting the report into print and partly from the length of time that material stays on library shelves and booklists. Tutors also tend to recommend books that suit their viewpoint, that they possess, have found useful in the past or have written themselves. This combination of inertia, bias, sentiment and even greed accounts for the need to examine the date of publication in relation to developments within subject disciplines.

Ageing is not the only danger. Books are reprinted frequently but revised rarely. A look at the publication or revision date is essential. Furthermore, publishing is a slow process. There is often an eighteenth-month delay between an article or a book being accepted and coming into print. The author's introduction will often give the date of completion and this is sometimes appended to an article in an academic journal. However, the lapse of time between completing the typescript and finishing the research has to be added. Fieldwork for the National Mobility Inquiry started in 1972. The manuscript was completed in 1978 and the two books were published in 1980.[24] *Social Relations in a Secondary School* was first published in 1967, based on fieldwork between 1963 and 1964.[25] Lacey's *Hightown Grammar* was published in 1970.[26] An article on the work appeared in 1966.[27] The fieldwork started in 1963.

When the lapse of time between fieldwork and publication is added to the time a book or article stays on the library shelf or on booklists, the world has often become a very different place. The books will often contain evidence from a previous era. The world is not static, but the evidence available in print often is. Examining student essays in education can be a trip down memory lane. The child development references are often from the 1920s. The studies of single schools by Hargreaves and Lacey remain firm favourites in the 1980s even though they were researched when secondary schooling was selective. The tendency for foreign authors to be translated late and for the classic nineteenth-century authors to be re-published adds to the confusion. Most of Durkheim's works first appeared in English in the 1950s and he is often treated as if alive and well in the 1980s. Marx also remains forever young as more obscure works are translated.

Behind the dating of evidence lie the changing models of human behaviour and organisation. At the surface the words change. Haberdasher, mannequin and wheelwright were still used in tests of reading for monitoring national standards in 1970–71. Being high and gay then was different from today. But more important was the changing context within which the evidence presented received its meaning. The invisibility of women was one example. We can look back and see how books and articles were focused on men. Across the two editions of this book the continual reference to 'he' and 'his' has been dropped. Even more important, the first edition in 1972 never considered the sexist bias in the evidence criticised.

The Controversy over Sir Cyril Burt that introduced this chapter is a warning of the rapidity with which the models behind the print can change. Books written before 1950 assumed that intelligence tests measured innate ability, that intelligence was fixed at birth. As it could not be changed by education it was recommended that children be divided into streams and given a separate curriculum to prepare them for their different stations in life. Today, the Norwood Report published in 1943 is derided for incorporating this view and for recommending secondary schooling based on it. But it was seen as progressive in its time. Burt died in 1971 and it took five more years for the fraud to be recognised. Books written within the last decade still contain elements of the model that divides children at birth and organises schooling to keep them in their predicted place.

The importance of the date of publication can be best illustrated through considering the changes in the models used to organise schooling in a multi-cultural society. Across twenty years from 1965 there have been three changes of model.[28] Thus the average life of a book before redundancy has been about five years. Yet early in this section this was shown to be the time needed to complete fieldwork and publish it. Books on multi-cultural education tend to be redundant as they are published.

The first stage prior to 1965 has been described as 'assimila-tionist'. It has a long history. The black presence was on the periphery of British culture, largely through the colonialisation of Asia and Africa. Most books incorporated images of the superiority of the European. Immigrants were expected to adjust and if possible assimilate. They were strangers with problems and their cultural deprivation needed to be overcome. Thus, the Plowden Report of 1967, still the definitive official statement of policy in primary schooling, has only 5 out of 555 pages on 'Children of Immigrants'.[29] It confirms D.E.S. Circular 7/65 that immigrant children should be dispersed so that no school has more than a third of such children. It is mostly concerned with their problems.

From about 1965 into the early 1970s there was an 'integrationist' stage. The racist tone in pre-1965 publications was replaced by the idea of tolerating cultural diversity. But the model was of the integration of black cultures into dominant white norms and values. Books published at this time stressed curricula that would help merge black culture into the mainstream. Across the 1970s the model changed to multi-culturalism. It was assumed that Britain had become a 'culturally plural' society. This is reflected in D.E.S. documents on the school curriculum in the early 1980s where the co-existence of cultures is stressed, and the need for all schools to reflect this in their curriculum emphasised. That is the message of the Swann Committee reported in Controversy 10.

The speed of these changes made it very difficult to keep up in print. But the upsurge of the 'anti-racist' model in the 1980s made all previous work look like tokenism. Now the emphasis was on *racism* and the unequal distribution of power that secured it. This view was incorporated into criticism of the Swann Report because it ignored the built-in racism of schooling. The Inner London Education Authority's *Race, Class and Sex* policy for racial equality in 1983, with its stress on rooting out racism from schools and on building awareness of it into the school curriculum, is a different world from that in the Plowden Report only sixteen years before.[30] In between were two contrasting models. Taking any book off the shelf was an invitation to redundancy.

Pressures on the author

Researchers rarely remain detached from their subjects. A look at Mead's biography *Blackberry Winter*,[31] or at Coffield's *Growing-up at the Margin*[32] shows the affection that comes from observing and participating. There are pressures too from the need to impress funding agencies, senior colleagues and publishers interested in sales. Authors also press their own views and favourite causes. In education there are pressure groups supporting comprehensive and public schools, streaming and de-streaming. These groups are vocal, organised and eager to produce results that will support their case. The obvious clues are to be found in the publishers or sponsoring bodies. Political parties and societies, religious organisations and pressure groups publish or sponsor useful but slanted books and pamphlets. This information is often on the title page or in the preface. It is worth while to get to know the views of some of the associations with the largest output. Thus the Fabian Society in supporting the collective solution to social problems and the Institute of Economic Affairs in its support for private enterprise are pressing particular political beliefs though they may claim only to approve publications and not to influence the authors. The *Critical Quarterly* and the *New-Left Review* find no difficulty in accumulating evidence to support their conflicting cases.

Even where there are no obvious sources of bias, there is still a need to study the professional and social pressures on the author. No scientist can escape these pressures, for the natural sciences require increasingly large sums of money and this tends to deflect research into channels approved by government or industry. Many eminent American social scientists joined Project Camelot after it received 6 million dollars from the US Army.[33] This was later terminated by the President of the United States when its objectives and political implications became suspect. Among the motives for joining was the attraction of belonging to a wealthy project close to the centre of power, a hope that the US Army could be humanised and deflected into constructive work, and even an honest admission that the money was good. But the cost of association was the taint of involvement in a project which was concerned with uncovering data on the causes of revolutions, for use by the US Army.

A more important restraint comes through controls exercised over individuals by the discipline of their subject. Undergraduate and graduate education immerses the student in books, lectures tutorials and research procedures that are chosen and controlled by teaching or supervisory staff. Getting a place and a grant for a second degree or to do research usually means fitting in to the field of interests of existing faculty members. Getting an article published depends on the attitudes of established men who act as editors or referees. In this way each subject exerts control over its members and it becomes a discipline. Hagstrom has argued that within scientific communities in the natural sciences any disputes that do arise are limited by the actions of those controlling publicity, so that the majority remain working in areas where there is agreement and students are given an image of unified contents and procedures.[34]

Some ideas of the conventions governing science can be gauged from Merton's view that the stress in science on advancing knowledge puts a premium on original contributions.[35] Rewards go to those who discover first, not only in the form of Nobel prizes, but through giving a name to a substance or process, thus bestowing immortality on men like Boyle, Mendel, Pavlov and Zeigarnik. This emphasis on originality often clashes with the other main stress in science on organised scepticism and objectivity. For most scientists, getting into print is a sufficient reward, symbolising originality, even if the reality was a routine report. The urge to publish is a result of the pressure on scientists to prove their ability to produce original ideas. The nearer to the frontiers of knowledge a scientist works, the greater is the pressure to succeed and the vulnerability of the individual to failure. The involvement of scientists with their peers is therefore a source of tension as well as of support.

Authors also write books from a viewpoint that is inevitably coloured by their own political ideology. An account by I. L. Horowitz of his reasons for writing *Revolution in Brazil* shows how the honest social scientist recognises this.[36] Horowitz was anxious to write a book about Brazil that did not contain the bias of many that had gone before. His own liberal view, transcending a purely nationalist perspective, led him to concentrate on areas of Brazilian life that had been of little interest before. But this was nevertheless a selection, honestly admitted to be a reflection of his own political views. A rare English example is Ford's expression of her socialism and hopes for an end to the system of stratification in Britain in her preface to her book *Social Class and the Comprehensive School*.[37]

For most of human history thinkers who have supported unpopular views have been silenced by those in authority over intellectual life. The worst modern example occurred in Soviet Russia under Stalin. From 1929 bourgeois elements in science were under attack. In 1936 the Medico-Genetical Institute was attacked in *Pravda* and then closed. In 1937 Lysenko, with support from Stalin, branded his opponents as deviationists and his own theories replaced classical, Mendelian genetics. Leading opponents were arrested and Vavilov, the leading Russian geneticist, was arrested, sentenced to death and actually died in prison in 1942, the year he was elected to the Royal Society.

The final triumph of Lysenko came in 1948, when hundreds of scientists were dismissed from their posts, had their degrees removed, were shadowed by the secret police and arrested. Books were removed from libraries and all teaching of Mendelism banned. From 1948 to 1952 Lysenko was supreme in Russian biology.[38] He was the only scientist to be called great in his lifetime. At his first lecture at the Agricultural Academy, staff as well as students attended. A brass band played as he went to the rostrum. The State Chorus had a hymn honouring him.

During this period discoveries abounded. They became increasingly absurd, but the support of Stalin and then Khrushchev was sufficient to silence critics. However, from 1952 a counter-attack developed. At first it concentrated on detail without openly criticising Lysenko. But the damage done to Russian agriculture finally weakened Lysenko's grip on Soviet science until attempts were made to effect a compromise with classical genetics. By 1963 open attacks were appearing and the advances of Western biology could no longer be concealed. Khrushchev resigned in 1964 and Lysenko was dismissed in 1965.

The lessons of the Lysenko tragedy support the case for continuous scepticism in science as well as continuous replication to test claims. A combination of circumstances helped Lysenko attain power over more distinguished scientists. His claims seemed to offer practical solutions to Russia's problems in agriculture. He was able to align his theories with the current political ideology and obtain the support of Stalin and Khrushchev. By branding his opponents as deviationists, spies and saboteurs he clawed his way above them. In a centralised scientific community all training could be rapidly adjusted to the new doctrine.

Nevertheless, it was not just the ability of the secret police to silence opposition that accounted for this triumph of pseudo-science. Under the conditions in a dictatorship that maintained that its ideology was itself scientific, the sceptic was a heretic to be liquidated. The claim of the Russian leaders that Marxism as interpreted by them contained the key to all problems, including those tackled by scientists, meant there could be no dispute allowed with the official Party line. The grip was tightened by centralised control over all the possible means whereby critics could publicise their views. Furthermore, potential critics were isolated from the community of international scientists who might have supported them. It was not only biology that suffered from the political accusations of the Party leaders, but also the other natural sciences and all those subjects that study man which were flourishing elsewhere during this period.

The Lysenko case is an extreme example of the interference of government in science; similar, if less extreme, cases could be found in the witch-hunting during the McCarthy era in the United States in the first half of the 1950s. Once the direction of scientific activity is dictated from outside the scientific community, and once the allegiance of scientists is to governments, a source of scientific reliability is sacrificed. The drive of individual scientists to get the recognition of their fellows and the granting of this recognition only after agreement has been reached about evidence by established scientists may have undesirable effects, but does guarantee that fraud is unlikely to pass and that professional competence will be required before acceptance is accorded.

It is not only in totalitarian regimes that scientific activity has been controlled for political purposes. American and British scientists have lost their jobs because of their political beliefs. In 1970 there was a typical example of the suppression of a report attacking the established policies of a scientific community. A long discussion paper prepared by Huberman for Unesco was ordered to be destroyed by the Director General.[39] From surviving copies it is evident that this destruction was aimed to stop the circulation of a swingeing attack on the conventional policies of this agency and in education generally. Such book-burning has occurred periodically in history in a variety of different religious and political climates. Less obvious, but more general pressures come from colleagues, editors, censors and organisations providing the money for research. Furthermore, the public listens to, and buys, what it wants to hear and read. It is easy to pander to this self-satisfying taste and inhibit the distasteful and unpopular. The published is always selected.

Individual scientists are not only influenced by state policy and the views of agencies providing the money, but by their own personal ambition. Robert Hooke, a prolific inventor, was forever contesting with men like Newton and Huygens about who had invented things first. Cavendish, Watt and Lavoisier all claimed to have first demonstrated the compound nature of water. Sir Humphry Davy opposed the election of Michael Faraday to the Royal Society because he maintained that Faraday's discovery of electromagnetic rotation was not original.

A remarkable illustration of the mixture of personal ambition, determination to beat rivals and scientific inventiveness has been provided by Watson's account of his work with Crick on the structure of the D.N.A. molecule.[40] The book also demonstrates how an author unconsciously puts himself at the centre of events and of the creative process. The search for a model of this molecule that would satisfy existing knowledge was being sought in many places. Crick and Watson felt the pressure of competition as they neared their solution and feared that one of the other groups concerned would come up with a successful solution first. The discovery was seen as one which would qualify for a Nobel prize. While this account probably leaves out the more mundane work and the real expertise of those concerned, it is a startling revelation of the motivation of scientists working around the frontiers of knowledge.

The scientist is therefore under pressure to establish his or her prior claim. As a consequence it is usual in the journals of natural sciences to publish the date of receiving manuscripts. This is the case with most journals of psychology but unusual in sociology or education. The relation between originality and recognition also appears in the tendency to use the number of publications as a measure of accomplishment. The urge to publish and the recognition of genuine originality are part of the same tradition, though they may have little else in common.

There are rare instances where personal ambition seems to have led to fraud. The history of science is littered with deliberate deceptions and sincere fallacies, and the line between the two has often been difficult to draw. One of the most famous cases of this type was the discovery in 1911 of the Dawn Man of Piltdown by the amateur geologist and archaeologist Charles Dawson.[41] The support of Arthur Smith Woodward, a noted scientist, overcame most of the contemporary doubts about the reliability of the evidence. Although the remains did not fit in with other contemporary evidence and were to stay isolated phenomena the few doubters were not listened to. In 1913 digging and sieving exposed other remains and in 1915 Dawson found more remains of a second Piltdown man. The anticipated evidence of man's ape-like ancestry seemed to have been found. Dawson died in 1916 and no further remains were found. *Eoanthropus dawsoni* existed as an anomaly. By 1948 new techniques had showed that the Piltdown skull was not more than 50,000 years old. Next, parts of the skull were shown to be of different ages and constitution. Then staining was detected and the teeth were shown to have been filed down. The jaw was shown to be that of an orang utan. Implements found near the skull were shown to have been recently shaped and stained and most of the fossils found nearby were frauds. This was a forgery that had been the work of a professional, skilled enough to convince some of the most august scientists of the time. It may have been an elaborate joke, an attempt to obtain fame or a deliberate fraud. The important point is that such evidence had been expected and was sufficient to convince not only the public, but leading scientists of the time.

In both the natural and social scientists energy has been wasted. Great effort has gone into proving the obvious and probing the trivial. The commitment of scientists to their community can blind them to the futility of their work. But where the alchemist could waste little but his own time, modern scientific enterprises can absorb fortunes. Project Mohole seems to have started as a way of boosting the prestige of the earth sciences.[42] It was established as part of AMSOC, the American Miscellaneous Society, which had been founded as a comic contrast to established scientific societies. The object was to bore a hole deep into the earth's crust. But accurate costing, specific objectives and sound organisation were neglected amid professional envy and political chicanery. Estimates rocketed from 5 to 125 million dollars. In the end the project was stopped by Act of Congress in 1966. Significantly, this action followed articles in journals reporting science to the public in an intelligible way. Science, secure within communities, can easily obscure its shortcomings from the public.

THE SWANN REPORT AND THE POLITICS OF RESEARCH

Controversies 1 and 9 have been concerned with the nature–nurture debate. The geneticists have often adopted racist positions, maintaining the inferiority of Jews or blacks or non-Aryans. Within education that debate merged with a practical issue over the education of immigrants in the 1960s. By the end of that decade, evidence of low attainment among newly arrived blacks had been collected in the Inner London Education Authority.[1] Since then, the cause of that low attainment and the implication of a multi-cultural society have become controversial issues.

The existence of low attainment among blacks raises a series of questions leading from the status of the evidence to the values held by those who act upon it. First, there are questions about the tests and examination results selected. Second, there are questions about the reliability and validity of those measures and in particular about bias in favour of white, anglo-Saxon males. Third, there are questions about the contribution of social class factors to evidence on ethnic groups. There are questions whether the reason for the low attainment lies within the children, or in their social or cultural background, or in the schooling they receive. Finally, there are questions about the policies that are needed, for these could involve changes in the organisation of learning or support a 'multi-cultural' curriculum on one hand or an 'anti-racist' approach on the other.

These issues came together in the publication of the Swann report in 1985.[2] Its title, *Education For All*, summarised its main conclusion that the problem is not in the education of ethnic minorities but of all children in a now pluralist society. It had been a troubled committee since it was established in 1979. Anthony Rampton, its first chairman, was asked to resign in 1981. Ten other members resigned during its life. The surviving members were informed by letter that they could collect their copy of the 800-page report at the same time as the Press. The final rumpus came when they read in this letter that Lord Swann had himself written a summary without consulting them. Two long-serving members expressed their alarm.[3] This was justified. The *Times Educational Supplement* saw this summary as the 'Final row for troubled Swann'.[4] But the controversy rumbled on.

The Government quickly rejected many of the key recommendations of the Swann Report. 'Sir Keith moves quickly to kill key Swann recommendations' was a typical headline[5] (*TES*, 22.3.85, p. 6). But if Sir Keith Joseph thought the report went too far, many thought it had not even started to tackle the main problem of racism, in schools as elsewhere.

The National Anti-Racist Movement in Education (N.A.M.E.) concluded that Swann's summary was 'an exercise in dishonesty'.[6] It was 'misleading and mischievous and probably intentionally so'. Certainly it had been publicly disowned by some black members of the committee. The main report was also criticised. While it acknowledged the existence of racism it did not apply this to the education service itself. This point is crucial and was also selected for comment by the Commission for Racial Equality[7] and the Runnymede Trust.[8]

Swann acknowledged that racism, ascribing inferior characteristics to categories of people, existed, but failed to apply this to the schools. Yet, by 1985, that had become the main criticism of education by blacks. Selection, streaming, suspensions, choice of options, entry to examinations discriminated against blacks, yet were ignored in the body of the report. Racism itself was left out of Swann's summary. To N.A.M.E. the report released teachers, L.E.A.s, the D.E.S. and the Government from their responsibility to stamp out racism in the schools. The Swann Report was itself seen as racist in emphasising the problems of black children, but not the problems of racist teachers.

10

THE PUBLICATION OF RESEARCH

So far the focus of this book has been on research and researchers. But evidence has to be prepared for publication. Once published it will be used by others. It will be read by most people in secondary sources. At each stage in the transition from original report, to articles, to books, to readers, to use by other authors there will be pruning and reinterpretation. The academic will be made practical and evidence given meaning in one discipline will be removed and used in another. All the questions asked of documents in Chapter 7 have to be asked of articles and books in current use.

There are two stages in publication that raise problems of reliability and validity. First, the researcher, knowing that academic peers will scrutinise the work, prepares the strongest case possible. Second, the evidence, once published, will be taken over by others to support their theories, often by applying it to areas not even envisaged by the researcher. Primary sources need to be interpreted in the light of Parts 1 and 2 of this book. But secondary sources have another weakness. The original researcher has lost all control. Whether disinterested or appalled at the treatment of their work by others after publication, researchers can do nothing about it. Readers should remember this loss of control.

The preparation and presentation of evidence

The cautions that need to be exercised in reading published accounts of research should first be directed at the preparation and presentation of evidence. It has already been argued that there are no free-standing 'facts' but only data from observations, or questions, or measurements that are made meaningful when related to some implicit or explicit theoretical model. In the human sciences in particular there are competing models and reference of data to these will produce different interpretations. Each will also be affected by the personal and political views of the author. Let the reader beware. Intepretations result from the need to make choices between ways of analysing data. But they range from careful management of the presentation of evidence to outright fraud.

Technological supercharging

Most senior social scientists, now surrounded in their work by computers and visual display units, started their statistical treatment of data years ago on the backs of envelopes. Punched cards, sorted by inserting a knitting needle, speeded this up but still left hours of work to produce even elementary statistics. The calculator accelerated this. But the real breakthrough was the computer. At first it too worked from punched cards. Now data can be accessed directly into a desk-top machine programmed to process it.

There remains the Garbage-in, Garbage-out problem. Easier data-processing does not remove any of the technical difficulties identified in Part 2. Samples can still be unrepresentative. Questions can suggest answers, and ethnographers will still see what they expect. The computer does nothing to improve validity and the easily produced statistics can conceal weakness with volume. Thus, Rutter and his colleagues (Controversy 2) related the input characteristics of the children, the way learning was organised in the schools, and achievements at leaving.[1] The statistical techniques related process factors such as the setting of homework or starting lessons on time, to output measures such as examination results, while adjusting for intake differences such as verbal reasoning scores at age 11. The technique used, log linear analysis, is complicated and the statistical tables and accompanying description are hard going even for statisticians. Goldstein reviewing this analysis concluded that they do not encourage the reader to place a great deal of confidence in the author's results.[2] But he is an expert in taking results apart. There is an Appendix in

Fifteen Thousand Hours written for the lay person, but its algebra is formidable.

Computerisation eases the production of statistics. It is impressive to read that results are significant at the 5 per cent level. But that only means that the possiblity that the statistics presented have occurred through chance in the selection of the sample are five in a hundred. Furthermore, that rather comforting figure depends on there having been a genuine sample, and, to some statisticians, one that is genuinely random.[3] That is rare in social research. For example, comparisons are often made between schools or classes in schools to see if different curricula or teaching methods produce different results. But teachers and L.E.A.s will not allow children, or classes, or schools to be randomly allocated to this curriculum or that teaching style. Technically, significance tests should not be used where existing classes or schools are compared even if they are carefully matched to ensure that like is being compared with like.

Fifteen Thousand Hours contains warnings about the need for caution over the interpretation of significance tests. Yet they are presented, and the twelve schools were not a random sample. Furthermore, authors select the significant and non-significant relations to be published. Others might have been equally informative not necessarily confirming the existence of strong school effects. Finally, statistical significance has no necessary relation to educational significance. This works two ways. Statistics can be presented as significant which have no practical relevance. But other educationally important relations may be left out because they are not statistically significant. For *Fifteen Thousand Hours* it has been argued that insistence on an arbitrary 5 per cent significance level enabled the authors to ignore a tenable counter-hypothesis that differences between schools could be explained by physical and administrative features, and by parental choice.[4]

Window dressing

There are two cosmetic conventions in the reporting of social research. One wraps the package in jargon. The other ribbons it with references. Both are legitimate targets for scepticism. Both secure a veneer of academic respectability to inferior material. This is not necessarily intentional bamboozling. There are conventions for reporting that locate published work in context for the appropriate scientific community. They are familiar with the conventions. But the lay reader may confuse shorthands, jargon and references for confirmations of reliability and validity, or alternatively reject it all as mumbo-jumbo.

The rejection of research by teachers can be gauged from the title 'Don't Talk to me about Lexical Meta-analysis of Criterion-referenced Clustering and Lap-dissolve Spatial Transformation: a consideration of the role of practising teachers in educational research'.[5] This rather desperate view reflects the urge to understand and benefit, coupled with frustration at the language used. Mitchell[6] from a headteacher's position and Drysdale[7] from the administrator's confirm the anxiety of those who want to be able to use research. But the position is not all gloom. Those accusing research of obscurantism have themselves completed higher degrees by research and have often been involved in 'teacher as researcher' projects.[8] Because research has become part of academic qualification and has influenced important 'gatekeepers' such as inspectors, advisors and senior teachers, its influence is often indirect and diffused, and consequently not dependent on academic articles. But there is a cost in this diffusion. Control over the evidence is lost and it is often removed from the theory that gives it meaning.

The most serious consequence of lapsing into jargon is that the words can be dressed up as explanations. Alienation is a description of discontented youth, not an explanation of it. To suggest that blacks do not do well at school because of low self-concept merely transfers the question to what causes this problem. Attributing poor working habits in a child to a lack of achievement motivation is to label not explain. Only when the terms are referred back to the models in which they have meaning is there the start of an explanation.

Particular attention is necessary for words linking figures. The distortion here has come to be called the 'fully-only' technique. Differences are described as 'fully' X per cent when the objective is to show a relationship, but 'only' X per cent when the aim is to suggest that no relationship exists. There are many common variations on this ploy. 'Twenty of the samples were selected for detailed study' usually means that the others did not look promising if the results were to confirm the hypothesis and were ignored. 'Typical results are shown' probably means that the best were picked out. 'Correct within an order of magnitude' may mean it was more wrong than right.

Another popular technique could be called stage army mobilisation. Here it is implied that the results presented are backed up by all the other researchers who matter. 'It has been long known that' may mean it has just been thought out. 'It is generally believed that' may mean that few others have speculated along the same line. 'The results are in line with major studies in this field' means that the point has been a matter of dispute. In some cases the mobilisation is predicted. 'The need now is for further research', 'Much additional work will now be required for full understanding' and 'the research will continue as resources become available,' all mean that the author does not understand the results, but is looking for a new grant to carry on trying.

Finally, the written account can be wrapped up in the conventional language of science labelled by Watkins as didactic dead-pan.[9] Scientists report their work in an impersonal, stylised manner that suppresses personal opinion and experience. Technical language is used to give the impression of absolutely reliable methods, unaffected by the personality and social life of the scientist involved. Scientists stage-manage the impression they give to their public.

References for prestige

The legitimate use of references is to alert the reader to the existence of relevant work that illustrates and supports the point put forward by the author. It acts as a shorthand to those who share a discipline, summing up whole areas of evidence with a single name. First, the references are selected to support a viewpoint and secondly they can become ends in themselves. An absence of references is suspicious, but so is a surfeit. The first possible misuse of references to look out for is over-abundance. When every line is littered with '(Smith 1960)' or '(Brown 1961)' the suspicion is that the author is boosting his case. The second misuse is the mobilisation of famous names to

144 The Limitations of Social Research

place the work on a par with the established. Dedicating the book to Hans, Talcott or Basil, writing it in memory of Bertrand, acknowledging a debt to Noam can serve the same function as a Soviet tribute to Stalin as the greatest scientist and Lysenko as his greatest disciple.

Such a muster of names also protects the author from criticism. Anyone on first name terms with the great and who acknowledges how much he owes to the advanced seminar at Harvard, is unlikely to be the target of critical hatchet men. Furthermore, filling the work with references to the established increases the chance of getting it published as the referees used by journals and publishing firms will see no harm in further publicising their work. In a small specialism within a subject publishing its own journal, a few on the inside refer to each other while those trying to get in have to distribute their references diplomatically to get their work accepted. Oldcom found a correlation of 0.96 between footnote references to the chairman of the doctoral committee and the successful completion of 100 Ph.D. dissertations.[10] The reference is a neat way of combining flattery with erudition.

The second ploy is the use of the obscure and exotic. No one is likely to look up references to the Revista Iberoamericana de Seguridad Social and there are abstracting services which enable the author to find unlikely examples. Better still are references to unpublished Ph.D. theses in obscure foreign universities who are loath to let anything leave their archives. Another variation to look for is a concentration on long foreign-sounding names. Smith and Brown sound like amateurs compared with Raskolnikov and Skavar. The Vienna School is more impressive than the Department in Birmingham.

The third target should be the ingratiating truism. 'As Kilroy has conclusively shown, orphans have no parents', is a model of many attempts to flatter. A fourth ploy to detect is the professional trump. Here the reference indicates to the reader that he or she does not share the company that the author keeps and therefore cannot challenge the written account. 'Participants at the recent congress in Bokhara will confirm' neatly places the reader outside the jet-set pale. Another variation is to refer to verbal communication or correspondence, preferably with some august academic. The palm goes to Taylor whose reference to Guzzetti in an address to the

D.E.S. 'Better Schools' conference in 1985 turned out to have everything in the way of didactic dead-pan mixed with the exotic and uncheckable. In the printed version it turned out to be 'Guzzetti, B. J. (1983) "A Critical Synthesis of School Effectiveness Research: Implications for Dissemination". Paper presented to the Northern Rocky Mountain American Educational Research Association, Jackson Hole, Wyoming (mimeo)'.[11]

Fraud, fallacy and fancy

Controversy 9 outlined the fraud uncovered in the work of Sir Cyril Burt. It was mainly concerned with the failure of the community of psychologists to act, as evidence mounted of Burt's unscrupulous activities as editor and researcher. Fixing results is rare, but there are a range of misleading interpretations of evidence. A well publicised example was an article by Wiggins and Schoeck, 'A profile of ageing: USA'.[12] The old were reported to be in good health, energetic, independent and secure within families or communities. This supported the opposition of the American Medical Association to free care for the aged. Yet investigation of the survey on which the profile was based showed that it had been loaded to produce the results and that non-whites in particular had been under-represented.[13] Ironically Wiggins and Schoeck were the authors of the previously published *Scientism and Values* warning against doctoring research to boost its credence.[14]

Fallacies occur when the level at which the data are analysed does not match the model guiding the research and used in the conclusions. Thus critics of Bennett's *Teaching Styles and Pupil Progress* argued that if the individual children rather than the school class had been taken as the unit of analysis, results may have been very different.[15] Similarly, Coleman relied on the verbal ability scores of his 645,000 pupils, distributed among 4,000 schools.[16] But to interpret overall school performance from the aggregated scores of children on a single test is to ignore features of schools that are more than the sum of those pupil scores. Similarly, it may be misleading to draw conclusions about individuals from measures of collective behaviour such as crime, birth or migration rates. Criminal statistics are a poor base for statements about individual motivation to commit crime, just as a knowledge of the motives of individual suicides is an inadequate source of information about the morale of a nation.

Alker details eight fallacies that are possible in analysis.[17] Riley has added two more where, although the actual research fits the theoretical model, the analysis sticks so close to a single level that information necessary for full understanding is concealed.[18] Psychologistic fallacies occur where a researcher ignores facts about social groupings in explanation. Sociologistic fallacies occur where information on individuals is ignored. Thus, psychologists have tended to ignore the uniformity and predictability of suicide rates while concentrating on individuals' states of mind, while sociologists have been contented to generalise from suicide rates and ignore the insights from studies of those who tried and failed.

A similar shift in level of analysis often occurs in the study of organisations and the roles of individuals within them. Sociologists are concerned with the structure, but to explain the effect on the individuals concerned fall back on psychological concepts such as internalisation and alienation. Thus, role is used by the sociologist as behaviour which individuals occupying a particular position feel constrained to follow. But to explain why individuals actually behave in a predictable, regular way there is a switch to explanation in terms of the effect of the role on behaviour. The focus is on the organisation and data is collected with this in mind. But the individual is linked to this organisation by assumptions about individual personality and behaviour. The consequence has often been a picture of men in organisations as passively responding to pressures rather than active and often disruptive participants.

The most common flaw is the production of broad conclusions from narrow evidence. The researcher starts with a hunch, collects data that may only be vaguely related and ends with certainty. The creativity has become fanciful. In these cases the connection between the evidence and the conclusions is often tenuous. For example, *Learning to Labour* by Willis,[19] or the same author's *Profane Culture* [20] are full of observations that grip. The sexist, racialist views, the acceptance of the work ethic and its intimate connection with masculinity, and the arrogance and even confidence of these working-class adolescents are vividly reported. In *Learning to Labour* the adoption of such views is shown to be a form of self-condemnation. It explains how working-class lads get working-class jobs. The reference is to the capitalist class system. But there are no references to social class, to alienation, to hegemony, to the other concepts used in the analysis within the first, descriptive part, largely contributed by those studied. The second part is only loosely derived from the first and in parts seems to contradict it. As Musgrove has pointed out in a review of *Profane Culture*, the groups studied are first described as apolitical, unaware of class oppression and exploitation, and then interpreted as selecting, developing and transforming their environment to make their own distinctive culture.[21] In one part they are seen as unconcerned with the institutional structure of society, and in the second as concerned with transforming it.

Another example is Riesman's *The Lonely Crowd*, a best seller in social science, half a million copies having been sold of the paperback version published in 1954.[22] Larrabee saw this popularity as a symptom of an urge to national self-analysis in the USA at this time.[23] The personality types suggested as paramount in different historical periods have become part of the language of sociology. But there is doubt over the interpretation of contemporary life that was presented. Riesman and Glazer, looking back after eleven years, admitted that they had serious misgivings about their thesis even before publication but decided to go ahead.[24] They admitted overestimating the degree of social change and the links between character and society. They also admitted that their analysis was incomplete, leaving out particularly such factors as the distribution of power which they later saw was crucial in understanding contemporary America.

The use of evidence in secondary sources

Once a work is in print the researcher waits anxiously for its reception. Articles in an academic journal have usually been refereed and responses from readers are often invited. It is the loss of control if the media get interested that can become a nightmare. Wild studies a town of 2,500 in New South Wales.[25] He moves there and gets the local paper to publish a description of the work he will be doing for his doctorate. Three years later his PhD thesis is ready and he converts it into a book, carefully changing all names to ensure anonymity. Lawyers work with him to cut out libellous bits. When the book appeared, journalists were not that easily fooled. The headlines in the newspapers soon announced 'THE BOOK THAT SET A TOWN AFIRE'. Wild writes an apology in the local newspaper. But soon he is taking part in a film of the book and looking back is pleased that he has exposed the pretensions of the 'bosses' and members of the Rotary Club.

In a similar way, it is usually easy to identify schools, factories and so on used in published case studies. But breaks in anonymity are not the only worries. Researchers are often appalled by the interpretations put on their work. Ford is mystified by the reception of her book on comprehensive schools.[26] They accuse her of omitting that which was included and including that which was omitted. Barker Lunn, having produced a closely-reasoned and neutral report on streaming for the National Foundation for Educational Research, finds it used to support conflicting cases and concludes that the users had either not read or not understood the book.[27]

The interest here is not with the use of evidence by the media or the public, but by other academics. First there is exampling, where snippets of evidence from here and there are extracted and cobbled together to present a case backed by research. Second, there is simplification, often multi-stage, whereby evidence is doctored until it is reduced to everyday language and applicable to everyday situations. This book incorporates all of these manoeuvres. Readers should be wary. Third, there is decontextualisation, where evidence is taken from its discipline and used in another or to make practical recommendations.

Exampling and simplification

Most books and articles in the social sciences and education are secondary sources, borrowing evidence to support a case. Here we are outside Popper's science as the search for the case that refutes. Little Red Books, Black Papers and White Papers can present simultaneously conflicting views of the same issue by selective exampling of the same evidence. Any book on a current issue in education will illustrate the ease with which evidence can be mobilised to support or attack progressive schooling, streaming, multi-cultural education and so on.

The hundreds of contradictory books on the teaching of reading would be amusing if this was not so important a subject for teachers, parents and children. Fortunately they take little notice of the experts as they attack each other. The problem for the reader lies in the ease with which evidence for one of the phonic or one of the holistic methods can be presented. The dogmatism of many writers seems odd when reviews of research in reading fail to find any one approach superior to any other. But that never inhibits anyone pressing their case for their methods, in any subject despite the failure of researchers to identify any teaching style or organisation that is more effective than any other in such a complicated activity as learning to read. The realism of that apparently pessimistic conclusion lies in pointing to the optimistic complexity, individuality and ingenuity of children and teachers as they interact with each other and with others outside the school.

The rise and fall of the Initial Teaching Alphabet (ita) is a good example of the dangers of readily accepting evidence. Phonotopy, printing by sound, was designed by Isaac Pitman in 1837. Sir James Pitman re-designed it and pressed for its introduction in England in the 1950s. Evidence from the Reading Research Unit in 1963 using controlled experimentation confirmed that use of ita was significantly beneficial.[28] By the late 1960s some 10 per cent of schools were using ita in Britain as well as in the USA. By this time the Schools Council had funded an independent evaluation by Warburton and Southgate.[29] This exposed the design faults of earlier research, much of which was funded by the ita Foundation. As usual when there is an independent evaluation the results were inconclusive. Supporters and critics launched into print to claim that this evidence supported their case. However, the fall of ita in the 1970s was as rapid as its rise in the 1960s. There may have been 2,000 schools using it by 1970.[30] By 1980 it was difficult to find any that had continued. It had fallen out of use and out of the debate among experts. In areas like the teaching of reading where expert passions run high it is best to sleep on the evidence for about ten years.

Decontextualising

In education, as in other enterprises to improve the human lot, social research is used as a basis for practical decisions. A lot of weight from half-a-million teachers can be placed on evidence that will support current practice. Textbooks tend to imply that primary school teachers feel the spirit of Rousseau over their shoulder and Froebel at their elbow as they struggle to get the reception class settled down. The movement to a liberal, child-centred education has been a blessing. But the continuous search for evidence to confirm this approach in the classroom has led to some very dubious beliefs. The problems arise once the evidence is taken out of its context within scientific disciplines. If theories determine research designs and the interpretation of evidence, removal from that context will be likely to undermine the conclusions drawn. In the original articles there is usually sufficient detail on methods to allow the key questions in this book to be answered. Once translated into a book on teaching, absorbed into official policy or lecture notes, the meaning of the evidence and its limitations tends to be lost.

An example is Susan Isaac's accounts of child development based on her work at the Malting House Garden School in Cambridge.[31] This is still quoted in most books on pre-school education. But the detail in the original account is usually ignored. The children in that school were very bright and often very disturbed. Many of their fathers worked in the university and the children left to go on to progressive public schools such as Bedales or Dartington Hall. It was a strange choice for conclusions about the maintained sector. It was even stranger as a major source for promoting freedom of opportunity and choice in early childhood education. The attraction was that Susan Isaacs systematically observed and recorded the behaviour of the children in the schools. But as the evidence was used so it was distorted.

Malting House Garden School is described as full of thirty little children very concerned with their sexual organs or lack of them. Little boys under three talk fearfully about their penises and their fear of losing them. One holds on to his nose as reassurance against possible castration. Little girls coming into the school where nudity seems to have been encouraged enviously observe the boys in the toilets. When this evidence is taken out of the Freudian model which gives it meaning, it is laughable. The highly selected thirty are odd examples for the normal child. Their behaviour is not just described by Isaacs but interpreted. Using this as evidence is to mistake that interpretation for value free 'fact'. My use of this example is absurd because I see Freud as yet another nineteenth-century figure modelling individuals as incapable of controlling their own lives. These accounts have meaning only inside the Freudian model. Outside they are barmy.

Across the twentieth century the movement to a developmental, child-centred education has grown in strength. As social science was established so it was used. In the early part of the century Freud was often exampled to show the benefits of permissiveness. But as the child-centred primary school movement gained momentum, Piaget became the major influence. He published *The Language and Thought of the Child* in 1923.[32] Until his death in 1980 he was a dominant figure in developmental psychology. But he remained a biologist steeped in the evolutionary view, seeing cognitive growth as the unfolding of a biological programme. That growth could not be accelerated. To Bryant, Piaget was 'bleakly negative' as an influence on education, seeing young children as incapable of logical thinking.[33] How then did this work come to be the intellectual support of progressive primary schooling?

The clue to Piaget's influence is that he took no direct interest in education and rarely commented on the use being made of his work. His first research was on the mollusc in 1911 and he still referred to this evidence in books published late in the 1970s. His conclusions were typical of scientists steeped in the nineteenth-century tradition. Cognitive development was an unfolding. The driving force was biological and the process evolutionary. Education could be organised to support this, but the rate of development was pre-determined and could not be accelerated. Children went through stages of cognitive development from sensori-motor to formal operations.

It is odd that this model was so attractive in supporting progressive primary schooling. The Plowden Committee for example used it extensively to encourage teachers to provide stimulating classrooms but not to try to teach children to read or calculate before they were 'ready'.[34] The idea of 'readiness' is referred to Piaget's stages. It was used to fix the age of transfer to secondary schooling and determined the case for middle schools, because secondary teachers were seen to assume that children were capable of abstract, formal operational thinking. Too early transfer would mean that children were not 'ready' for this. In retrospect this seems pessimistic. Yet it gave teacher educators an academic basis for their work. Piaget was an intellectual giant, productive for over fifty years. By careful exampling and simplification his work could be used to support the notion that learning not teaching was important. Child-centredness, informal learning and play were features of Froebelian and other approaches to early childhood education. Piaget seemed to give these a modern psychological basis. But this meant fudging the association of chronological age with Piaget's stages. By the early 1970s, the idea that young children could not reason in an abstract way was under challenge. By the late 1970s babies were shown to be thinking logically.[35]

Donaldson has used recent research, testing some of Piaget's theories to demolish the idea that children under six or seven are egocentric, incapable of perceiving events from any but their own viewpoint.[36] Piaget's experiments with young children may not have made sense to the children. The nature of the experiment, not the capacity of the child, may have determined the results.

This is not merely of theoretical interest. The notion that there was a stage below which children were egocentric meant that they were not seen as capable of deductive reasoning until they were six or seven. Yet Donaldson reports many experiments setting the same tasks but in ways that made sense to the children where they could infer from one set of conditions to another by abstract thought of the 'if A is greater than B, and B is greater than C, then A must be greater than C' type. Here one early repeat of Piaget's experiment using an altered design will be used to illustrate what happens when a cornerstone of education is chipped away.

In 1971, Bryant and Trabasso reported that their experimental work showed that young children could make transitive inferences, thus refuting Piaget's conclusions.[37] Following hard on the publication of the Plowden Report and on the publication of many books that assumed the reliability of Piaget's work it was bound to be news. The press seized on the Bryant and Trabasso replications and headlines in *The Observer* of 'Children scupper Piaget's Law' were followed elsewhere by reports of Piaget's theory being undermined and by forecasts of major changes in teaching methods.[38] The *Daily Telegraph*, after reporting that the educational world would never be the same again, went on to predict that primary school teachers could now get down to teaching rather than minding fun parties.[39] These reports, in line with the political leanings of the papers concerned, turned out to be based on a telephone call from an *Observer* reporter to Bryant.[40] Inevitably there was dispute over what he actually said when he complained that he had been misinterpreted.

There is little doubt that the popular version of undermining and scuppering will pass into educational folklore. The *Observer* article that sparked off the controversy appeared on 22 August 1971. The Bryant and Trabasso article had appeared on 13 August 1971, but in *Nature*, a journal not usually read by those interested in discussing education.

It still has to be explained how Piaget's work, focused on his own and other children in Geneva, not primarily concerned with education, came to be chosen as the intellectual basis for teacher education in the 1960s. The explanation probably lies in the distance between his original work, written in French and concerned with biology, cognition and epistemology, and tips for teachers. At each stage in the adaptation the practical relevance was boosted as the methodological weaknesses were forgotten.

First, the original work had to be translated. It remained tough-going. So a third level industry adapting it to psychology began under titles such as *The Developmental Psychology of Jean Piaget*[41] or *Piaget's Theory of Cognitive Development*.[42] Applying the work to education generated an even more flourishing industry. Here are ten titles published between 1955 and 1973: *Some Aspects of Piaget's Work,*[43] *Piaget's findings and the teacher,*[44] *A Brief Introduction to Piaget,*[45] *Piaget: Some Answers to Teacher's Questions,*[46] *A Teacher's Guide to Reading Piaget,*[47] *An Outline of Piaget's developmental psychology for students and teachers,*[48] *A student's guide to Piaget,*[49] *Piaget for Teachers,*[50] *Piaget in the Classroom,*[51] *Piaget sampler*.[52] The last four were published after the evidence attacking Piaget was in the academic journals. This industry also produced a second level publication entitled *Children's Ways of Knowing: Nathan Isaacs on Education, Psychology and Piaget*, in honour of the man who produced two of the ten booklets.[53] Translated, exampled, simplified and decontextualised, Piaget provided the intellectual prop for the progressive educationalists in the 1960s and 1970s, just as Freud had done earlier in the century. The message is in retrospect clear. Better to be sceptical of the great and good while they live than adjust to their demolition after their death.

DO TEACHING STYLES AFFECT PUPIL PROGRESS?

In April 1976, Neville Bennett and his fellow researchers in the University of Lancaster published *Teaching Styles and Pupil Progress*.[1] Few books have received such media coverage. It hit the national press overnight. The *Times Educational Supplement* distributed copies to reviewers in advance so that in the issue on the Friday following publication there were central page spreads of summary, comment and criticism.[2] In each of the major journals there were extended reviews and articles. The authors counterpunched their critics with vigour. There were television and radio broadcasts, questions in the House of Commons and in education committees.

The furore can only be understood by the timing of the book. 1976 was a critical year for education. It was the year of the William Tyndale school enquiry, the House of Commons Expenditure Committee's report on the attainments of the school leaver, the Yellow Book prepared by the D.E.S. and the Prime Minister's speech at Ruskin College. All these events were symptomatic of what has since been described as the start of *Schooling in Decline*.[3] Significantly it was also the year when expenditure on education stopped growing and when falling rolls hit the intakes to secondary schools in city areas. The Lancaster research on primary schooling was dropped into this debate with aplomb by a new publishing firm. That 10,000 copies were sold on the first day was not surprising.[4] Neither was it surprising that this turned out to be the classic educational controversy over research findings. The academics slugged it out to the joy of editors. Some concentrated on the study itself. But much wider issues were raised. Thus, from one corner Miller applauded Bennett for researching into something of practical importance, and attacked critics for their lack of action and surfeit of theorising.[5] In the other corner, McIntyre pressed for researchers to report only to people who were technically competent to evaluate their work.[6] Bennett's shortcomings were not seen as confined to technical incompetence, but to trying to communicate with teachers about matters that were beyond them.

The *Times Educational Supplement* of 30 April 1976 ran three pages of reviews.[7] These were neatly balanced, one hostile from two American researchers, one uncritical from a headmaster and one guarded by a researcher. But it also included comments from Rhodes Boyson and the Confederation for the Advancement of State Education.[8] The former saw the work as breaking the conspiracy of silence surrounding progressive primary schooling, while the latter were surprised that parental influence was not considered. These appeared with brief comments from Bennett under the headline 'Dr. Bennett shrugs off Black Paper Connection'. Gray, later to emerge as leading hatchet man, also reported that his own research had produced different results. On 7 May the *TES* gave a background report on the publishers of the book and Gray gave more details of his own research.[9] Sinha added a letter, pointing out that his college of education had produced two of the research teams including Bennett, that they were indeed child-centred in their view, but that this did not indicate indoctrination by himself or fellow tutors.[10] On the 14 May, Clegg returned to England and wrote to ask what the fuss was about.[11] De Bono also took the opportunity to link Bennett's evidence to his own interest in the teaching of thinking.[12] On the 21 May, Bennett and Entwistle replied to their critics.[13] This was a technical counter-attack, but also accused the critics of innuendo and inaccuracy. Predictably on the 28 May Walker published a letter under the heading 'Such a silly debate',[14] and Hughes another under 'It's just common sense'.[15] The *TES* wound up the debate on 4 June. There was a three-page centre-spread from Bennett, Bruner, Entwistle, Marsh, Owen and Rogers.[16] Gray also wrote that his contribution three issues before had been misunderstood in Bennett and Entwistle's response a fortnight later because the *TES* had left out part of his evidence.[17] Unfortunately this had made it seem that his evidence supported rather than opposed that of Bennett. Fortunately, the *TES Scotland* had published the full text, giving the Celts the chance to see what the Sassenachs had missed.

A similar series of reviews and letters appeared in *New Society*. Here, however, Bennett was more fortunate for Bruner wrote a very favourable review.[18] He was indeed enthusiastic enough to have also written the introduction to the American version of the book. The major technical criticism in *New Society* came from Satterly.[19] All the major educational journals later carried extended reviews. The most enjoyable were in *Educational Research*. Here Gray and Satterly joined forces to contribute 'A chapter of errors: Teaching Styles and Pupil Progress in Retrospect'[20] which stated: 'Given a research design that is so flawed it is doubtful whether any meaningful conclusions can be drawn from the study.' Bennett and Entwistle soon followed with 'Rite and Wrong: A Reply to "A chapter of errors" '.[21] Neatly they suggested that Gray and Satterly had written prematurely in the heat of the popular furore, as well as being wrong, performing a rite and mis-stating the conclusions of the book. The knockabout fun was in danger of obscuring the importance of the debate.

As usual in these controversies, the reviews became balanced once the temperature cooled. *The Harvard Educational Review* of 1977 not only carried two lengthy articles, but the Atlantic divide enabled these reviewers to point to two factors; selection at 11 years and the strong influence of parental occupation on attainment in Britain that should not have been ignored.[22] But by this time the evaluations of Follow Through, the successor of the Head Start programmes, were partially supporting Bennett's conclusions about the benefits of formal styles and his evidence could be put into a wider context.

There is no point in reproducing the technical dispute over *Teaching Styles and Pupil Progress*. They are well documented and the data are still being reanalysed. But one aspect is important. Much of the criticism revolved around technical points which probably made little difference. But there were less technical design decisions that could have been very influential. The most obvious was the way the teachers were categorised into formal, informal or mixed styles. Twelve categories were identified, not by observing teachers in action, but by their perception of their own style. Of these twelve categories 1 and 2 were grouped as 'informal, 3, 4 and 7 as 'mixed' and 11 and 12 as 'formal'. Now there is clearly a problem in collapsing categories in this way. Many factors which could make up the package that defines degree of formality were ignored. The teachers could have practised very different styles to those they professed. They probably varied their styles between classes, groups and individual children. The 'mixed' category does seem a rag-bag. The important point is that there were only twelve teachers in each of the three 'styles' and small errors in allocation could have had large effects on the results. There was also a sampling problem among the pupils. There may have been some 400 per teaching style, but results for types of pupil are reported for as few as four pupils in one type, and discussions of high and low achievers in different types of classroom sometimes refer to less than ten children.

The criticism of Bennett has to be placed in the context of the task he set himself. It was important to produce evidence to supplement that already in existence. All attempts to find what is involved in effective teaching have failed so far. No research has identified the features in teachers that can raise pupil attainment. It is doubtful whether any prediction from teaching style to pupil progress would pay off. There are so many factors inside and outside the school that we even have to debate whether schools have any effect. The choice may be to go on trying, with the risk of producing frail evidence, or to contract educational research to private communication between academics. My own view is that research evidence is one kind among many. It is the responsibility of researchers to produce it, to secure the maximum reliability and validity, publish it, but not to claim superiority over evidence collected by teachers, advisors, inspectors and so on. It is different, not superior, in the criteria used for validation. Its claim to respect is that the methods used are not only tried and possible to replicate, but that they are published for others to answer the key questions which introduced this book. In this sense the controversy over Bennett's research was part of the way evidence should be assessed for credibility.

The furore eventually led Bennett, to his credit, to cooperate in a re-analysis of the data under the direction of Aitken (1981).[23] The first focus was the clustering of teachers into formal, informal and mixed styles. Common sense suggests that no teacher would fit perfectly into any one. Aitken used a different technique to cluster into three styles best fitting the teachers in the sample. The formal group turned out to be similar to Bennett's. But Aitken's informal group contained a different set of teachers. Even more serious his group were not Bennett's 'mixed', but largely the inconsistent and unsuccessful. The only sensible conclusion from these discrepancies is that clustering statistically on the basis of answers to questionnaires has dubious validity.

Aitken's second focus was on pupil progress and its relation to teaching style. The problem lay with Bennett's assumption that there was no variation among the teachers within the three styles. Once Aitken took this into account all the statistically significant differences in the effect of the styles on pupil progress disappeared. These contrasting results should not be accepted as necessarily refuting the original conclusions. Aitken's technical, low key publication in an academic journal has not received the critical surgery on Bennett's more sensational book. The episode raises important questions about the difficulties of researching into the effectiveness of teaching and the problems of publication. This was an important topic. It should have been researched. Once published it was bound to be of public concern. But how can you build in sufficient warnings about the reliability and validity of the data so that the media will not sensationalise? To Hesketh, one of the team engaged for the re-analysis under Aitken, the need is for 'open, verifiable, honest and thorough' studies.[24] But even if these are achieved the media and the public may still ignore technical cautions. Even if they respect them, later writers will use the results to support their case. The academic soon becomes polemic.

This debate over the impact of teaching on attainment has been moved on by the ORACLE project.[25] This team see their work as a refutation of Bennett's. They rejected the use of questionnaires for classifying teachers and relied instead on observations in classrooms. The result is a more sophisticated classification of teaching styles. The responses of children adopting different learning styles is then used to see how teachers affect children's attainment (Galton and Simon, 1980). This is still open to the criticism that it gets nowhere near the complexity of the real situation.[26] But it is an example of the way conceptualisation becomes increasingly sophisticated. Bennett (1976) classifies teachers on the basis of questionnaires.[27] ORACLE reject this as too crude and use observations in classrooms. Further, they also classify children's learning styles. But Bennett returns to the scene in *The Quality of*

Children's Learning (1984) to argue that observation is insufficient.[28] This has to be followed up by diagnostic interviews to ensure that overt behaviour was not concealing the real meaning of events to teachers and children.

Bennett et al. 's The Quality of Pupil Learning Experiences is an intensive attempt to see how teachers organise learning tasks for 6- and 7-year-olds, and how these children respond to them. Teachers were interviewed before the school day started to get a picture of the tasks for the day. Children were observed while working and then interviewed. This is sensitive work. The observers were all experienced teachers given an 'intensive training'. They not only had to observe, but simultaneously formulate hypotheses explaining why individual children ran into difficulty or found the work easy and think out tests to follow these up. These hypotheses were then tested during the diagnostic interview that followed. This is real grounded theorising however vulnerable. Bennett's point is valid. Only by getting some idea of the way children understood the tasks and then probing during interviews could the meanings they had given to the teachers' efforts be understood. Other studies depending only on observation may have taken performance in the class as a reflection of the meanings assigned. Bennett's evidence suggests that this is not the case even with these young children. When teachers set high level intellectual tasks the children were not fooled. They knew that what teachers really want are not deep thought and problem-solving, but plenty of good writing and pages of sums correctly and neatly produced.

This Controversy illustrates all the limitations of social research. There are problems in the theoretical models of teaching and learning. This inadequacy has made it difficult to design research, collect and analyse data in a reliable or valid way. The disputes end inconclusively because the models used cannot reflect the complexity of real learning situations, and the statistical techniques cannot compensate for this deficiency. Publishing the results means pruning the methodological cautions and the consequent critical battle is too late or too technical to affect the use of the results for political purposes.

11

THE SCOPE AND LIMITATIONS OF SOCIAL RESEARCH

The limitations of social research are usually attributed to technical weakness in design, data collection and analysis described in Part 2. That is not just mistaken because it fails to consider the creative activities that precede and follow the technical stage and described in Parts 1 and 3, but because the models used, implicitly or explicitly, account for the design and for the interpretation of the evidence. The sources of limitations are now summarised. Marking out the boundaries of a subject, defining the limits of its applicability and determining the line beyond which reliability and validity fall fast, also yields the area within which there is strength. The scope as well as the limitations are being defined.

Conceptual limitations

There are two limits imposed by the difficulties in modelling human behaviour and organisation. The first arises from the complexity of the human condition and the ingenuity of individuals in breaking free of any constraints on development, interaction and individual behaviour. The second is the consequence of this ingenuity. It has swung social science from the search for laws of observed behaviour to the search for the meanings that individuals give to events.

Part 1 of this book was concerned with theoretical difficulties. In each social science there are a variety of competing models. Each gives contrasting explanations. The adherents of each describe different social worlds and hence recommend conflicting ways forward. The contemporary dispute in economics between the monetarist's view of economic life and Keynesians is an example.

Each models economic activity and recommends opposed policies to improve the wealth of nations. Psychology remains divided between behaviourists sticking to the experimental method and shunning consideration of unobservable inner thoughts and cognitive psychologists for whom thought processes are central. In sociology, Marxists and functionalists focus on structures and the way they constrain individuals, while social interactionists and phenomenologists look for the meanings given to those constraints by individuals as they overcome them. These divisions have always existed. Some models are top-down stressing structure, some bottom-up stressing individuality. The important point is that each theoretical model results in different ways of designing research, collecting and analysing data. Evidence is not free-standing, immutable and universal. It is bound into the model that produced it and gave it meaning.

The second limitation arises from the shift to interpretation in the social sciences. There is no doubting the strength of the criticisms of scientistic approaches, nor the excitement of getting to the way individuals see the world around them. Yet the technical weaknesses are obvious. That may be the price of the validity gained. Looking into everyday situations, writing accounts up in the language of those studied and avoiding pre-determined methods brings social science very close to media reporting, to literature and to the reports of professionals such as inspectors. Around its boundaries social science merges with journalism and prescription. The removal of the term 'Science' from the title of the Social Science Research Council was a recognition of this boundary problem.

This loss of the science label is welcomed by many who resent the grip of scientism on social enquiry. Once you get *Inside the Whale* of society it is not reducible to laws but requires imagination and metaphors that are not mechanical.[1] This can often be expressed as fiction. The acceptance of this view has been recent. As it involves the sacrifice of the title 'scientist' it has not been easy to accept. The 1970 conference of the British Sociology Association launched the 'new' Sociology of Education in Britain and was full of attacks on positivism. Yet the one paper from an outsider, by Bantock, pointing to the similarities between sociology and literary criticism, was unwelcome.[2] The conference papers have all been published in a number of books. But Bantock's contribution has always been excluded. Now this view that the boundaries of sociology overlap with fiction has become academically respectable.

Technical limitations

Part 2 of this book covered the technical difficulties in collecting data on human activity. These techniques make up the main content in most books on social science methods. These encourage the view that the important step is to select means of collecting data. Yet it was just this emphasis that led to the rejection of scientism. Once in the field with questionnaire, interview or observation schedule, the more sensitive researchers realised how divorced they were from the really important social events, how much was lost or distorted through sticking to the techniques, and how artificial was the picture drawn by the statistics summarising the riches of social interaction.

Looking back to reports of research undertaken twenty years ago is often embarrassing. Here is an experiment reported in a book still recommended for most courses on early childhood education. Harrold and Temple (1959–60) studied forty-two children from four infant schools, half having had previous nursery schooling.[3] The children in the two halves of the sample were matched for intelligence, age and social background and then given a variety of tasks while observed by the researchers. Those having previous nursery school experience were shown to be happier, more self-confident and at ease with teachers in their infant classes. They were 'better' in every respect except painting and manipulative control. They were also superior in muscular development, social relationships and attitudes to parents. Even the finding that they were more aggressive is taken as an advantage of receiving nursery schooling. Yet the degree of control in this work gives no confidence that the results were not the outcome of the expectations of the researchers and the teachers questioned. In the 1980s the data from such a study of forty-two children would result in pages of computer output and significance levels. But the technical limitations would remain the same. The reader has to be sceptical because there is little control over the techniques used or the researchers' expectations, and little consistency between each successive piece of research. Above all, it ignores the processes through which the influences could have worked, ignores the interactions this involved and ignores the children as active participants.

Lack of control in social research applies to the researchers as well as the techniques they use. Questions are adjusted, asked in a different tone. Bias enters observations and the personal feelings of the researcher influence the data recorded. The readers of reports of such research rarely have any guide to the allowances that have to be made. As a guide there is a report, titled 'Unleashing the untrained' on the fieldwork of ninety-eight anthropology students in California.[4] The tutor of this exercise describes the consequences as 'methodological and ethical violence'. The researchers pursued their data with a blatant disregard for the rights of others, giving away confidences, reporting illegal practices, obtaining information by fraud and breaking promised anonymity. They peeped into privacy and stirred up an industrial dispute. Cheerfully, the organiser of this debacle concluded that they had irreparably damaged the chances of any further research in this area.

Organisational limitations

There are two limitations arising from the organisation of social research. First, there are the personal, professional and political hopes of the researchers that can influence not only the topics chosen for investigation, but the way this is organised and the results interpreted. Second, these researchers work within scientific communities that have established traditions and maintain these through managing the rewards available to the ambitious and the funds for research.

Once it is accepted that research is designed through the adoption of theoretical models, the possibility of bias is obvious. If the theory is to be grounded in the data as they are collected, the scope for bias is further increased. At least in these cases there is acknowledgement that a theoretical position underpins or arises out of the data. In the best of research this position is spelled out. But the reader is often left to guess how much the evidence reflects the preconceptions of the researcher as distinct from those of the researched. There will also be preconceptions arising from the researcher's political views. In all social research the views of researchers are influential. They are engaged in a social and political process. Much of Part 2 spelled out the consequences of this interaction during data collection, while Part 3 was concerned with the way the author's views affected the results presented.

The rejection of the role of neutral observer by researchers is often the result of getting into the field, not only of holding strong political views beforehand. Anthropologists can 'go native' once beguiled by the charms of the simple life. Evaluators of social programmes are often so appalled by the conditions they observe that they act to improve the situation not to study it. This is the real rejection of scientism. The objective of social research becomes the exposure of injustice and the overthrow of the arrangements that secure it. It is odd to read that capitalism lies behind the larking about of these comprehensive schoolchildren, but that is a shorthand for a situation where identifiable groups are getting a rough deal. This may be expected by the politically aware, but can also be the consequence of researching into real situations where the textbook discussions of inequality are met in their real, immediate, personal and moving form.

This shock during fieldwork is increased by the second factor in the organisation of the sciences that limits the scope of research. The subjects are organised into hierarchies. Attaining a position through qualification and promotion means meeting the norms established by seniors in the community. The traditions tend to be both authoritarian and scientistic. Both constrain researchers. The authority is exerted within the community to ensure that those promoted meet the standards defined by their seniors. But authority is also manifested in the subject matter of social research. This tends to be focused on the poor, the deprived, the powerless. It is top-down, rarely concerned with those with power and rarely challenging their right to hold it. That has been a recurring criticism of economics as well as sociology and anthropology.[5]

The most important manifestation of the top-down scientistic approach of social sciences that are organised into communities where promotion and publication are controlled, is to limit the innovation that is promoted during research as issues are met that do not fit conventional methods. Qualification is usually judged on scientistic criteria. Every student whether writing an essay or completing a doctoral thesis has felt this pressure. The methods used may satisfy examiners but they are not suitable for catching the topic. The brave may abandon the study and their career. Most adjust to conform to the standards required for qualification. There are accounts of those who broke out, but there are many more who worked on and produced another of Medawar's frauds, full of conventional scientific activity that is a carefully doctored account of often messy reality.[6]

Policy limitations

The final set of limitations come from the use made of social science outside academia, in guiding policy and activities such as teaching. The utilisation of social research is usually investigated in relation to policy making. Thus, Kogan *et al.* have studied the *Government's Commissioning of Research*, concentrating on the Department of Health and Social Security.[7] The evidence from social research is also used by students, teachers, journalists and many others as they look for a firmer basis than opinion in their work. Models of research utilisation fit the student or teacher searching for information as they do the role of the researcher in policy-making. Furthermore, the motive for using research evidence is the same in both cases. Decisions have to be made, but there is always a lack of information. Research is an important, available source. Even more important, its shortcomings are assessable through the type of questions seen as central in this book.

Weiss suggests seven models for looking at the impact of research.[8]

1. The classical, linear model wherein pure leads to applied research, which is then developed and disseminated.
2. The problem-solving model whereby a problem is identified and research contracted to guide requisite formation of policies.
3. The interactive model wherein a continuing dialogue between researchers and policy-makers replaces the linear sequence in 1 and 2 above.

4. A political model wherein research is sponsored and employed on the assumption that it will support the policy already adopted.

5. A tactical model wherein research is contracted to delay having to make a decision.

6. An enlightenment model wherein research permeates the policy-making process, often through indirect routes.

7. An intellectual exercise model wherein research is seen as one among many possible influences upon policy.

The clue to the usefulness of each of these models lies in the policy-making process itself. This is not a sudden coming together of the great and good to produce a policy that is then put into practice according to the book. It is rather a long process of formulation by many often conflicting parties. Similarly implementation is often unpredictable and liable to produce practices that bear little relation to the intentions of those who produced the policy.

This rather messy and certainly not rational or linear view of policy-making means that models 1 and 2 above are unrealistic, although they are those most frequently written about in books on research. As decision-making is cumulative, drawing on many sources and long drawn out, the enlightenment model (number 6) is likely to be the most realistic. This also applies to the use of research evidence by students, teachers and others making decisions about their own policies and practices. Research evidence percolates through to us through discussion, the media, lectures, popular as well as academic journals. Each of models 3 to 7 rings true at times. We have all disputed the validity of research (model 3), used evidence to boost our case (model 4), used it as an excuse for inaction (model 5) and placed it alongside recommendations from inspectors, lecturers and so on as one source of guidance (model 7).

The enlightenment model with its emphasis on the percolation of research evidence into decision-making and of generalisations into the way practitioners think about social issues increases the importance of sceptically reviewing the status of social research. It means that not only tailor-made but second-hand interpretations of evidence will be influential. It means that research of all qualities will filter through. It means that research results will be wholesaled by popularisers, journalists, and interested professionals. The 'consumers' will often not be aware of the source of the evidence or how far it has been distorted during the percolation. The importance of asking the four questions in the Introduction to this book becomes more important as it is appreciated that research exerts its influence in this indirect, diffused way.

Ignoring the limitations

If evidence feeds in to decision-making in a diffused way, there can be no sustained control over quality. Further, dubious evidence can exacerbate already sensitive political issues. Are there then some subjects where research, with all its weaknesses, is liable to do so much harm that it should not be pursued? In the case of racial differences in intelligence many social scientists would answer 'yes'. But the discussions of the Bennett research on *Teaching Styles and Pupil Progress*[9] (Controversy 11) and Rutter's *Fifteen Thousand Hours*[10] (Controversy 2) might also suggest that a combination of high profile and low validity makes misunderstanding inevitable. The counter-argument, that research may be fallible but is a base for later researchers to build is strong, but only if the public can be informed of the limitations before action is taken on the evidence.

Ignoring the limitations of social research rarely leads to decisions to withdraw from an area because of its political sensitivity. Far more common has been the tendency to extend evidence beyond the limits that its reliability and validity justify. When that confidence is combined with the attempt to answer questions of human motivation and development, the result has often been a fatalistic, deterministic social science allowing little room for individuality, ingenuity and enterprise.

Extending beyond the middle ground

Social science is strongest when it is concerned with modest theorising about available data. Speculation about the distant past and the future is exciting but the lack of control puts its status as science in doubt. That also applies to natural scientists. Piltdown

Man was accepted as genuine for forty years by palaeontologists, because it fitted their model. Scientists refused to accept the possibility of aeroplanes even after the Wright Brothers had flown because it did not fit theirs.

Yet the potential for prediction is a measure of a science. Boyle's Law enables us to predict that if the pressure on a gas is increased while the temperature remains constant, the volume will decrease. When predictions get longer-term or more ambitious or are beyond controlled experimentation with easy repetition, the natural scientists can go haywire. The distinguished Canadian astronomer, Professor J. W. Campbell, in a paper entitled 'Rocket Flight to the Moon', in 1938, calculated on the basis of some odd assumptions that it would require a million tons of take-off weight to carry one pound of payload on the round trip.[11] As late as 1956, the Astronomer Royal asserted that 'Space travel is utter bilge'.[12]

This misplaced confidence of natural scientists that they can predict rests on the projection forward of existing developments and trends. The watershed in natural sciences was at the end of the nineteenth century. Nobody living before that time could have predicted accurately through the discovery of radioactivity, relativity, the uncertainty principle and so on. When the prediction is about humans it is more perilous, for we change our own future. If you doubt the power of individuals to do this, think of the stock market. Pundits predict trends, but individuals collectively defeat them. If accurate prediction were possible there would be no market.

Demography consists of the projection forward of present population trends. Over the short term this can be a sufficient for planning public and private services. Once humans are given opportunity to change the time when they marry and their sexual habits within it, demographers are in trouble. Gregory King, in his *Observations on the State of England* in 1696, predicted that it would take 600 years for the population of England, then about 5,500,000, to double. Today we top 47,000,000. In 1938, Charles predicted a population of between 18 and 32 million for Great Britain in year 2,000.[13] She left herself a wide margin, but we already have 56.5 million.

If prediction and even projection is perilous because humans make their own future, so is history, because what is left to study is usually unrepresentative. We tend to assume we can reconstruct across centuries. Archbishop James Ussher looking back in the seventeenth century concluded that the world was made in 4004 BC on 21 October at 9.00 am. Human scientists settled for a division of development, both social and individual, into stages. Evolution was in the academic air of the nineteenth century. Comte (1798–1857) produced a three epoch model of social development, Theological,/ Military to Metaphysical/Juridical to Scientific/Industrial. Spencer (1820–1902) postulated Simple to Compound, to Doubly Compound to Civilised. With a lawyer's brevity, Maine (1822–88) put forward status to contract. These were not just seen as models, but as natural and necessary sequences.

Psychologists took over this evolutionary thinking. Still very popular is Erikson's eight-stage view of human development, with each transition marking the solution of a crisis.[14] These crises, in sequence, are oral, anal, phallic, latency, puberty, early adulthood, late adulthood, old age. The Freudian influence is obvious. So is the failure to appreciate the anthropological evidence that contradicts such stages (see Controversy 3). What is not obvious is the status of the crises. Many a placid pensioner would not have noticed them. The most influential in education has been Piaget's four-stage model of cognitive development, from Sensori-motor to Symbolic/ Representational to Concrete operational to Formal operational.

Both predictive and historical errors can be minimised if the status of models is remembered. They are constructed from available theories, evidence and a lot of hunches. They are useful in getting a grasp on complicated reality and particularly for deriving further hypotheses for testing against reality. But they are not reality, are usually context-free, and are constructed for testing, improving and elaboration. They should never be given a status beyond that of the tentative. They also assume that there is enough known to produce the model. We are back with science as profitable when dealing with the soluble. When looking for a solution it helps to know the answer in advance.

Determinism

Determinism occurs in two stages. The first is to assume that everything has a cause. If two factors appear together or vary together they are assumed to be causally related. But there may be no link between them. Further, even if they are related, the direction of causality is usually difficult to determine. For example, the frustration–aggression hypothesis suggests that if children are pent up they will get fractious. But it is equally plausible that aggressive children are constrained more than their more docile peers. It is even more likely that third factors link both factors.

The second stage is to theorise that human affairs are determined by factors beyond human control. The Marxist flow of history driven by material developments sweeps us through class struggle towards the classless society. To Spencer, humans and their societies evolve organically, sweeping individuals along on an evolutionary tide. To Freud, human development starts with primitive urges that are finally controlled if never eliminated, just as human history has evolved from the savage to the civilised. Marx, Spencer and Freud who expressed these views were Victorians, seeing the world as developing through stages in a pattern over which individuals had no control.

This determinism remains at the heart of much social science. It assumes that everything that co-exists is related. The search is on for causes and these soon come to be expressed as binding. Attainment is seen as determined by social background. Intelligence is seen as given at birth through the genes. Each is deterministic. They co-existed in texts on education for over fifty years. The belief that all things are caused and that these are beyond individual control, was stronger than the common-sense that psychologists and sociologists could not both be right in holding these contradictory views. But they were both wrong in modelling mechanistically. Neither left room for the humanity.

Research and be damned?

The limitations outlined earlier raise questions about whether research into the genetic basis of intelligence, or even the incidence of low attainment among ethnic groups, should continue. The latter is among the terms of reference of the D.E.S. Assessment of Performance Unit, which has the task 'to seek to identify the incidence of under-achievement'. Yet proposals to organise the necessary research have been opposed. The problem lies in the relation of attainment to social class. Unless that can be taken into account, differences between different ethnic groups are likely to be the result of their class not their ethnicity.

The opposition to research on the genetic basis of intelligence is based on past experience as well as the technical difficulties of definition and measurement. Even if there were 'culture-fair' tests they will measure only a very limited aspect of intelligent behaviour. Controlling for the interaction of genetic and environmental factors only results in controversy over the attempt. By the 1970s the disagreements were so acrimonious that research had dried up. In 1969 Jensen reviewed the literature on racial and social class differences in intelligence.[15] This was followed by another issue of the *Harvard Education Review* devoted to critiques of his views and a further issue containing his replies to his critics.[16] With the explosive racial situation in the USA, Jensen's suggestion that there were innate differences in the distribution of measured intelligence between races was sure to cause an uproar. But three points stand out in the ensuing dispute. First, many thought the subjects should never have been investigated. Second, there were vitriolic attacks on the personal integrity of Jensen. Third, his standing as a psychologist was challenged. Similar criticisms were later made of his supporters in Britain.

The Jensen report was used by segregationists in the Southern States of the USA to justify existing inequalities in education.[17] Jensen, however, maintained that he was trying to develop a new theory of intelligence that would hold more hope for successful compensatory education, thus helping ethnic minorities. Brazziel, however, claimed that the *Harvard Educational Review* had acted irresponsibly in publishing evidence that would inevitably be misunderstood and used to sustain inequality.[18] Another critic maintained that to raise the issue at all was racism.[19]

In this dispute personal abuse was mixed with academic criticism. Jensen was likened to Governor Wallace, was accused of supporting the idea of negro inferiority and of justifying school segregation. When the National Foundation for Educational Research decided to include an article by Jensen in *Educational Research* it was attacked for its racialist content, but also for the pseudo-scientific nature of the evidence produced even before the actual article was published.[20] The validity of the evidence was challenged in advance. The National Foundation was accused of 'elevating a bogus and largely discredited thesis into respectability'.[21] The acting director of the National Foundation replied that it would have been prejudice and censorship not to publish a contribution from such a distinguished psychologist.[22]

More fuel had been added to this dispute by the publication in Britain of a book by Eysenck before the furore over the original Jensen article had died down.[23] Here a serious social and academic issue was virtually reduced to farce by the conflicting critics.[24] The author, a refugee from Hitler's Europe, was accused of Fascism. Methodological errors bordering on lunacy were suggested and terms like ignorant and impudent abounded. Eysenck was accused of playing into the hands of politicians, of disregarding the work of environmentalists and of being unscientific and unscholarly. Unfortunately, this apparent incompetence was seen to be combined with an effortless, masterly and persuasive style that would too easily capture the imagination of the intelligent plain man. Academic incompetence, a lack of personal integrity and a facility to seduce the public were seen as combined.

The only way the plain man can cut through this animosity is to wait until the original controversy has died down. Thus, Bodmer and Cavalli-Sforza in a calm review of the evidence over a year after the publication of Jensen's original article concluded that the currently available evidence was inadequate to resolve the question in either direction.[25] They agree that in the present climate of opinion the chances of misinterpretation of the evidence are so high that publication inevitably increased racial tensions. Above all, they saw many more useful biological problems for the scientist to tackle that could lead to more conclusive answers and more fruitful action.

The balanced view contrasts with the emotion generated earlier. First, there is no accusation of stupidity, personal malice or political reaction. When controversial subjects are investigated the scientist runs the risk of being labelled not only as a Fascist or a Communist, but as an imbecile. Second, the priority given to the research is judged against alternative possibilities, not against the political climate. The danger of accusing publishers of airing disruptive views is that it can lead to censorship. The liberal critics of Jensen and Eysenck were themselves under attack from more radical social scientists who saw the need, not to stop at criticism, but to convert social science into action against an unfair situation. With such diverse views the struggle might focus on who had the right to censor, not on the quality of the articles presented for publication.

Perhaps the most alarming aspect of this controversy was its value as news. It was reported in newspapers and popular magazines as well as academic journals. In all there was some discussion of the reliability of the methods used in collecting the evidence. This unusual concern with reliability occurs only when accepted views are challenged. It acts as another pressure on the scientist when choosing his research area. When the reward may be recognition by some colleagues and the hatred of others; when personal integrity, political belief and professional competence are likely to be discussed in public, and when brief, often distorted versions are to reappear through the mass media, the scientist is no longer a detached observer. It is a brave man who will expose his work to both the microscope and the hatchet.

However, there is no sign that the contestants in the nature–nurture dispute are shy of being involved in a public wrangle. Jensen ensured that the article which caused all the fuss in the *Harvard Educational Review* was available to the press in advance.[26] J. S. Coleman, whose analyses of White Flight were received as yet another attack on policies to achieve racial equality, is similarly prone to ensure maximum publicity. Eysenck carries on his arguments in letters to the national press. Indeed, he and Rose, the co-author of the National Union of Teachers pamphlet to counter the Jensen and Eysenck views, seem to produce a double-act whenever the issue comes into the public domain.[27]

After a searching review of the possible costs and benefits of continuing research in this area. Block and Dworkin conclude that it should not.[28] They confirm this view by looking at the distortion that inevitably follows research as it is reported in the media. Thus *Newsweek's* headline following Jensen's 1969 article in the *Harvard Educational Review* was 'Born Dumb?'[29] It went on to develop the idea of intelligence as fixed, not open to change and that blacks are born with less of it than whites. This misinterpretation is hard to avoid given the ambiguity in the academic articles on which the media stories are based. Black and Dworkin see misuse of the evidence as inevitable. There might still be a case for continuing the work, but there is little of scientific interest left in the nature–nurture debate. Given this, scientists are advised voluntarily to give up this line of enquiry. The political climate is too sensitive for it not to do harm. This is a reasonable argument and has support in the UK as well as the USA. Regardless of the rights and wrongs, it confirms the inevitable seepage of politics into social research.

The scope of social science

The limitations above also define the space left for social research to contribute to understanding the human condition and to inform policies and practices to improve it. Limits on our capacity to model reality and on the techniques for collecting information confirm Merton's support for 'middle range' theories confined in time and space where there is the possibility of dealing with real data from recent history or through investigations of contemporary life.[30] In an area such as social stratification and its consequences for education such a restricted horizon has been very productive.

Within this middle ground where theory and data can be related social scientists are at their best, probing into the gaps between what people think is happening and what actually occurs. This is the happy hunting ground, yielding the unexpected and the newsworthy. At one end are studies divorced from any political context. These secondary teachers may think that their classes are working normally, but Woods from the back of the classroom observes that a game is being played.[31] The children are 'having a laugh' to test out the teacher and establish limits to their authority. Those infant school teachers may see themselves as even-handed in their treatment of the children, but King sitting in the Wendy House sees them highlighting sex and class differences.[32]

At the other extreme is Willis on *Learning to Labour* (Controversy 6). Here the rejection of schooling by his sample of lads is explained as the consequence of capitalism. The school serves the state by ensuring that the lads take up manual jobs. Schooling is placed in its historical and political context. Researchers are concerned with the gap between what people think is happening and what the researcher sees is happening. But each starts from a different theoretical position. Woods adopts the interactionist perspective that teachers and pupils will interpret their experiences differently. Willis accepts this, but adds a Marxist view that the intepretations will be the consequence of ideologies originating in the class structure of capitalist society.

This focus on the gap between ideal and real, intended and unintended in the middle range is the exciting part of social research. It is also the important part. It is part of the 'demystification' that Rex sees as central to social science.[33] It may often be trivialised by taking events out of their historical and political context. But it can probe into the way organisations such as schools, or procedures such as social research, can, intentionally or not, reinforce injustice. Probing into the gap between intention and practice can show how even the evidence supporting that injustice is itself constructed from preconceptions that accept the existing structure of society as legitimate.

The exhilaration of, and motivation for, social science lies in this humane endeavour to improve the human lot. Social science is a haven for the curious, the alert, the detached and the non-conformist. This makes it even more urgent for social scientific communities to exercise discipline over individuals presenting new evidence. But the relevance of social science also requires not mystery but clarity in the picture presented to the public. Candour is needed to promote informed scepticism instead of naïve acceptance or rejection. This book was written to promote such scepticism. It should have been read in that spirit.

REFERENCES AND FURTHER READING

Controversy 1. The nature–nurture dispute

1. F. Galton, *Inquiry into Human Faculty and its Development*, Macmillan, 1883.
2. W. McDougall, *An Introduction to Social Psychology*, Methuen, 1946.
3. For a discussion of this Eugenics movement, see N. J. Block and G. Dworkin, *The IQ Controversy: Critical Readings*, Pantheon, 1976.
4. See, for example, J. M. Thoday, 'Geneticism and environmentalism', in A. H. Halsey (ed.), *Heredity and Environment*, Methuen, 1977, pp. 29–39.

Chapter 1. Scientific activity in practice and in theory

1. See for example J. Law and P. Lodge, *Science for Social Scientists*, Macmillan, 1984.
2. A. Cottrell, 'Science is objective', in R. Duncan and M. Weston-Smith (eds.), *Living Truths*, Pergamon, 1979, p. 179.
3. I. Firth, 'N-rays – ghost of a scandal past', *New Scientist*, 25 Dec. 1969, pp. 642–3; H. J. Eysenck, *Fact and Fiction in Psychology*, Penguin, 1965, pp. 127–30; I. J. Good, *The Scientist Speculates*, Heinemann, 1962, Index.
4. P. Medawar, 'Is the scientific paper a fraud?', in D. Edge (ed.) *Experiment*, B.B.C., 1964, pp. 7–12.
5. K. R. Popper, *Conjectures and Refutations*, Basic Books, 1963.
6. T. S. Kuhn *The Structure of Scientific Revolutions*, University of Chicago Press, 1962.
7. K. R. Popper, *The Logic of Scientific Discovery*, Science Editions, 1961.
8. Kuhn, *op. cit.*
9. E. Garfield, 'Negative science and "The Outlook for the Flying Machine" ', *Current Contents* **26**, 27 June, 1977, pp. 17–22.
10. *Ibid.*, p. 8.

Controversy 2. Do schools have any impact?

1. H. A. Averch *et al.*, *How Effective is Schooling? A Critical Review of Research*, Educational Technology Publications, 1974.
2. J. S. Coleman, *Equality of Educational Opportunity*, US Government Printing Office, 1966.

3. C. S. Jencks *et al.*, *Inequality*, Allen Lane, 1973.
4. M. Rutter *et al.*, *Fifteen Thousand Hours*, Open Books, 1979.
5. D. Reynolds, 'The search for effective schools', *School Organization*, **2**,3, 1982, pp. 215-37.
6. P. Mortimore, *The Junior School Project*, Inner London Education Authority, 1986.
7. See, for example, Radical Statistics Education Group, *Reading Between the Numbers*, BSSR Publications, 1982.
8. B. Tizard *et al.*, *Fifteen Thousand Hours*, Bedford Way Paper, 1980. E. Wragg *et al.*, *The Rutter Research*, University of Exeter, School of Education, 1980.
9. See, for example, J. Gray, 'Towards effective schools: problems and progress in British research', *Brit. Ed. Res. J.*, **7**,1, 1981, pp. 59-69 and H. Goldstein in Tizard, *op. cit.*, pp. 21-5.
10. T. A. Acton, 'Educational criteria of success', *Ed. Res.*, **22**, 1980, pp. 163-9. For response, see M. Rutter, 'Educational criteria of success: a reply to Acton', *Ed. Res.*, **22**, 1980, pp. 170-3. See also A. Heath and P. Clifford, 'The 70,000 hours that Rutter left out', *Oxford Rev. of Ed.*, **6**,1, 1980, pp. 3-19. For response see B. Maughan *et al.*, 'Fifteen thousand hours: a reply to Heath and Clifford', *Oxford Rev. of Ed.*, **6**,3, 1980, pp. 289-303.
11. Goldstein *op. cit.*
12. See 10 above.
13. P. Mortimore *et al.*, 'The ILEA Junior School Study', in D. Reynolds (ed.) *Studying School Effectiveness*, Falmer, 1985.
14. Rutter *op. cit.*, Bennett, see Controversy 11.
15. J. Gray *et al.*, *Reconstructions of Secondary Education*, Routledge and Kegan Paul, 1983.
16. See, for example, J. P. Willms and P. Cuttance, 'School effects in Scottish secondary schools', *Brit. J. of Soc. of Ed.*, **6**,3, 1985, pp. 289-306.
17. D. Reynolds and K. Reid, 'The second stage: Towards a reconceptualization of theory and methodology in school effectiveness research', in D. Reynolds (ed.), *op. cit.*, pp. 191-204.

Chapter 2. Interpretive social science

1. A. Calder, 'Mass observation, 1937-1947', in M. Bulmer, *Essays in the History of British Sociological Research*, Cambridge University Press, 1985, pp. 121-36.
2. See G. Easthope, *History of Social Research Methods*, Longman, 1974.
3. L. Humphreys, *Tearoom Trade*, Duckworth, 1974.
4. K. Lindsay, *Social Progress and Educational Waste*, Routledge, 1926.
5. J. L. Gray and P. Moshinsky, 'Ability and opportunity in English Education', in L. Hogben *et al.*, *Political Arithmetic*, Allen and Unwin, 1938.
6. J. E. Floud, A. H. Halsey and J. M. Martin, *Social Class and Educational Opportunity*, Heinemann, 1957.
7. D. Glass (ed.), *Social Mobility in Britain*, Routledge and Kegan Paul, 1954.
8. J. W. B. Douglas, *The Home and the School*, McGibbon and Kee, 1964. J. W. B. Douglas *et al.*, *All our Future*, Panther, 1968.
9. K. Fogelman (ed.), *Growing Up in Great Britain: Papers from the National Child Development Study*, Macmillan, 1983.
10. A. H. Halsey, A. F. Heath and J. M. Ridge, *Origins and Destinations: Family, Class and Education in Modern Britain*, Clarendon, 1980.

11. See, for example, R. Deem, 'Gender and social class', in R. Rogers, *Education and Social Class*, Falmer, 1986, pp. 173–91.
12. J. Seeley, 'The "making" and "taking" of problems', *Social Problems.*, **14**, 1966.
13. H. Roberts, *Doing Feminist Research*, Routledge and Kegan Paul, 1981.
14. L. Stanley and S. Wise, *Breaking Out: Feminist Consciousness and Feminist Research*, Routledge and Kegan Paul, 1983.
15. E. Durkheim, *Rules of Sociological Method*, Routledge and Kegan Paul, 1952.
16. A. Giddens, *New Rules of Sociological Method*, Hutchinson, 1976.
17. E. Durkheim, *Suicide*, Routledge and Kegan Paul, 1952.
18. See, for example, N. Anderson, *The Hobo*, University of Chicago Press, 1923.
19. See, for example, M. Shipman, *Educational Research: Principles, Policies and Practices*, Falmer, 1985.
20. C. H. McCaghy and J. K. Skipper, 'Lesbian behaviour as an adaptation to the occupation of stripping', *Social Problems*, Fall 1969, pp. 262–70; and J. K. Skipper and C. H. McCaghy, 'Stripteasers: the anatomy and career contingencies of a deviant occupation', *Social Problems*, Winter 1970, pp. 391–405.
21. H. Newby, *The Deferential Worker*, Allen and Unwin, 1977.
22. B. Stierer, 'Testing teachers? A critical look at the Schools Council Project *Extending Beginning Reading*', *Primary School Review*, **13**, 1982. See also V. Southgate *et al.*, *Extending Beginning Reading*, Heinemann, 1981.

Controversy 3. What really went on under the banyan trees?

1. M. Mead, *Coming of Age in Samoa*, Penguin, 1943.
2. G. S. Hall, *Adolescence*, Appleton, 1904.
3. S. Freud, 'Three essays on the theory of sexuality', in A. Richards, *The Pelican Freud Library, No. 7: on sexuality*, Penguin, 1977.
4. See J. Howard, *Margaret Mead: A Life*, Harvill Press, 1985.
5. See, for example, T. Parsons, *The Social System*, Free Press, 1951.
6. M. Mead *op. cit.*, p. 12.
7. D. Freeman, *Margaret Mead and Samoa*, Penguin, 1984.
8. M. Mead, *Blackberry Winter*, Angus and Robertson, 1972, pp. 178–80.
9. See, for example, J. and J. Ritchie, *Growing up in Polynesia*, Allen and Unwin, 1979 and L. D. Holmes, *Samoan Village*, Holt, Rinehart and Winston, 1974.
10. See, for example, M. Mead, *Letters from the Field, 1925–1975*, Harper and Row, 1977.
11. A. Bandura, 'The stormy decade: fact or fiction?', in R. E. Muus (ed.) *Adolescent Behaviour and Society*, Random House, 1971, pp. 224–31.
12. J. Grixti, 'Images of adolescence', *Universities Quarterly, Culture, Education and Society*, **40**,2, 1986, pp. 171–89.

Chapter 3. Interpretive social research

1. McCaghy and Skipper, *op. cit.* (ch.2, n.20).
2. B. Malinowski, *Argonauts of the Western Pacific*, Routledge, 1922.
3. P. Halfpenny, 'The analysis of qualitative data', *Sociological Review*, **27**,4, pp. 799–825.

4. R. G. Burgess, *Strategies of Educational Research: Qualitative Methods*, Falmer, 1985, pp. 8–10.
5. D. H. Hargreaves, *Social Relations in a Secondary School*, Routledge and Kegan Paul, 1967.
6. C. Lacey, *Hightown Grammar*, Manchester University Press, 1970.
7. S. J. Ball, *Beachside Comprehensive*, Cambridge University Press, 1981.
8. R. G. Burgess, *Experiencing Comprehensive Education*, Allen and Unwin, 1983.
9. N. Fielding, *The National Front*, Routledge and Kegan Paul, 1981.
10. R. Homan, 'Interpersonal communication in Pentacostal meetings', *Sociological Review*, **26**,3, 1978, pp. 499–518.
11. R. Wallis, *The Road to Total Freedom: A Sociological Analysis of Scientology*, Heinemann, 1976.
12. Humphreys, *op. cit.* (ch.2, n.3).
13. J. Ditton, *Part-Time Crime: an Ethnography of Fiddling and Pilferage*, Macmillan, 1977.
14. S. Henry, *The Hidden Economy*, Robertson, 1978.
15. G. Mars, *Cheats at Work*, Allen and Unwin, 1982.
16. C. Fletcher, *Beneath the Surface*, Routledge and Kegan Paul, 1974.
17. M. Hammersley, 'The researcher exposed: a natural history', in R. G. Burgess (ed.), *The Research Process in Educational Settings*, Falmer, 1984, pp. 39–68.
18. D. Jenkins, 'Chocolate cream soldiers: sponsorship, ethnography and sectarianism', in Burgess *ibid.*, pp. 235–70.
19. Wallis, *op. cit.*
20. D. Gaiman, 'Appendix: a scientologist's comment', in C. Bell and H. Newby, *Doing Sociological Research*, Allen and Unwin, 1977, pp. 168–9.
21. R. King, *All Things Bright and Beautiful? A Sociological Study of Infants' Classrooms*, Wiley, 1978.
22. P. Woods, *Teacher Strategies*, Croom Helm, 1980.
23. P. Woods, *Pupil Strategies*, Croom Helm, 1980.
24. B. G. Glaser and A. L. Strauss, *The Discovery of Grounded Theory: Strategies for Qualitative Research*, Aldine, 1967.
25. M. A. Porter, 'The modification of method in researching postgraduate education', in R. G. Burgess, *op. cit.* (n.17), pp. 139–62.
26. G. Turner, *The Social World of the Comprehensive School*, Croom Helm 1983.
27. D. R. McNamara, 'The outsider's arrogance: the failure of participant observers to understand classroom events', *Brit. Ed. Res. J.*, **6**,2, 1980, pp. 113–26.
28. M. Hammersley, 'The outsider's advantage', *Brit. Ed. Res. J.*, **7**,2, 1981, pp. 167–72.
29. M. Galton and S. Delamont, 'Speaking with forked tongue? Two styles of observation in the ORACLE project', in R. G. Burgess, *Field Methods in the Study of Education*, Falmer, pp. 163–90.
30. N. K. Denzin, *The Research Act*, Aldine, 1970.
31. C. Bell, 'Reflections on the Banbury Restudy', in C. Bell and H. Newby, *Doing Sociological Research*, Allen and Unwin, 1977, pp. 47–62.
32. M. Shipman *et al.*, *Inside a Curriculum Project*, Methuen, 1974.
33. H. Newby, 'Appendix: editorial note', in Bell and Newby, *op. cit.*, pp. 63–6.
34. P. Marsh, E. Rosser and R. Harré, *The Rules of Disorder*, Routledge and Kegan Paul, 1978, pp. 30–57.
35. R. Barrow, 'The logic of research: on ORACLE', *Durham and Newcastle Research Review*, **10**,53, 1984, pp. 182–8.

Controversy 4. Has Comprehensive schooling raised or lowered standards in education?

1. J. Steedman, *Progress in Secondary Schools*, National Children's Bureau, 1980.
2. For this and other examples see J. Dancy (ed.) *Childrens' Progress in Secondary Schools*, School of Education, University of Exeter, 1981.
3. *Ibid.*
4. C. Cox *et al.*, *Real Concern*, Centre for Policy Studies, 1980.
5. J. Steedman *et al.*, *Real Research*, National Children's Bureau, 1980.
6. Dancy, *op. cit.*
7. Dancy, *op. cit.*
8. British Educational Research Association, 'Statement by Executive', *Research Intelligence*, April, 1981.
9. J. Marks *et al.*, *Standards in English Schools*, National Council for Educational Standards, 1983.
10. *Times Educational Supplement (TES)*, 'Editorial', 1 July 1983, p. 2.
11. J. Marks and C. Cox, letter to *TES*, 8 July 1983, p. 4.
12. J. Gray, 'Questions of background', *TES*, 8 July 1983, p. 4.
13. J. Gray and B. Jones, 'Disappearing data', *TES*, 15 July 1983, p. 4.
14. A. Flew, letter to *TES*, 22 July 1983, p. 6.
15. J. Gray, letter to *TES*, 5 August 1983, p. 6.
16. J. Wrigley, letter to *TES*, 19 August 1983, p. 7.
17. *TES*, 'Editorial', 16 Dec. 1983, p. 2.
18. *Ibid.*
19. D.E.S. Statistics Branch, *Statistical Bulletin* 16/83, D.E.S., 1983.
20. J. Marks *et al.*, Survey of examination results in inner London secondary schools, reported in B. Hugill, 'ILEA secondaries under attack for exam record', *TES*, 25 April 1986, p. 3.
21. W. Stubbs and P. Mortimore, 'Principles and practices', *TES*, p. 2 and The Baroness Cox and J. Marks, 'Dismissal of data will not help ILEA under-achievers', *TES*, 6 June, 1986, p. 18.

Chapter 4. Sampling

1. H. Blumer, *An Appraisal of Thomas and Znaniecki's 'The Polish Peasant in Europe and America'*, Social Science Research Council, 1939.
2. C. Gipps and H. Goldstein, *Monitoring Children*, Heinemann, 1983, pp. 63–9.
3. D.E.S. Assessment of Performance Unit, *Science in Schools, Age 15, Report No. 4*, D.E.S. 1986 and *Science in Schools, Age 13, Report No. 4*, D.E.S. 1986.
4. D.E.S., *Primary Education in England*, H.M.S.O., 1978.
5. D.E.S., *Aspects of Secondary Education in England*, H.M.S.O., 1979.
6. D.E.S., *9 to 13 Middle Schools*, H.M.S.O., 1983.
7. D.E.S., *Education 8 to 12 in Combined and Middle Schools*, H.M.S.O., 1985.
8. R. G. Burgess, *op. cit.* (ch.3, n.8).
9. Galton and Delamont, *op. cit.* (ch.3, n.29).
10. F. Coffield, C. Borrill and S. Marshall, *Growing Up at the Margins: Young Adults in the North East*, Open University Press, 1986.
11. Hargreaves, *op. cit.* (ch.3, n.5).
12. A. C. Kinsey *et al.*, *Sexual Behaviour in the Human Female*, W. B. Saunders, 1953.

13. J. Hemming, *Problems of Adolescent Girls*, Heinemann, 1960.
14. For this and other blunders see L. Rogers, *The Pollsters*, Knopf, 1949.
15. Bullock Report, *A Language of Life*, H.M.S.O., 1975.
16. Warnock Report, *Special Educational Needs*, H.M.S.O., 1978.
17. Office of Population Censuses and Surveys, *General Household Survey, 1982*, H.M.S.O., 1984.
18. J. Gabriel, *The Emotional Problems of the Teacher in the Classroom*, F. W. Cheshire (Melbourne), 1957.
19. F. Musgrove, *Youth and the Social Order*, Routledge and Kegan Paul, 1964.
20. J. Newson and E. Newson, *Infant Care in an Urban Community*, Allen and Unwin, 1968.
21. J. W. B. Douglas, *op. cit.* (ch.2, n.8).
22. J. H. Goldthorpe, *Social Mobility and Class Structure in Modern Britain*, Clarendon Press, 1979.
23. Gipps and Goldstein *op. cit.* and D.E.S., Assessment of Performance Unit, *op. cit.*
24. T. W. Adorno *et al.*, *The Authoritarian Personality*, Harper Bros., 1960.
25. B. G. Glaser and A. L. Strauss, *op. cit.* (ch.3, n.24).
26. See, for example, M. Hammersley and P. Atkinson, *Ethnography: Principles in Practice*, Tavistock, 1983 and P. Atkinson and S. Delamont, 'A critique of "case study" research in education', in M. Shipman, *op. cit.* (ch.2, n.19), pp. 26–45.
27. Porter, *op. cit.* (ch.3, n.25).
28. A. D. Edwards and V. J. Furlong, 'Reflections on the Language of Teaching', in Burgess, *op. cit.* (ch.3, n.29), pp. 21–36.

Controversy 5. Terrorist or Resistance Fighter? The case of the football hooligan

1. J. A. Harrington, *Soccer Hooliganism*, J. Wright, 1968.
2. See Sports Council and S.S.R.C., *Public Disorder and Sporting Events*, Social Science Research Council, 1978.
3. S. Hall, 'The treatment of "football hooliganism" in the press', in R. Ingham *et al.*, *'Football Hooliganism': the wider context*, Inter-Action Inprint, 1978.
4. I. Taylor, ' "Football Mad". A speculative sociology of football hooliganism', in E. Dunning, *The Sociology of Sport*, Cass, 1971, pp. 352–77. See also I. Taylor, 'Hooligans: soccer's resistance movement', *New Society*, 7 Aug. 1969, pp. 204–6.
5. J. Clarke, 'Football and working class fans: tradition and change', in R. Ingham, *op. cit.*, pp. 37–60.
6. Taylor, *op. cit.* (1971).
7. P. Marsh, *Aggro. The Illusion of Violence*, Dent, 1978, p. 147.
8. Sports Council and S.S.R.C., *op. cit.*

Chapter 5. Studies based on observation

1. R. Rosenthal and K. L. Fode, 'The effect of experimenter bias on the performance of albino rats', *Behavioural Science*, 1963, pp. 183–9.
2. R. F. Bales, *Interaction Process Analysis*, Addison-Wesley, 1950.

References and Further Reading 183

3. M. Galton and S. Delamont, *op. cit.* (ch.3, n.29).
4. R. Homan, 'The ethics of covert methods', *Brit. J. of Soc.*, **31**,1, pp. 46–59.
5. L. Festinger, H. W. Riecken and S. Schachter, *When Prophecy Fails*, Harper and Row, 1956.
6. L. Davies, *Life in the Classroom and Playground*, Routledge and Kegan Paul, 1982.
7. O. Lewis, *Life in a Mexican Village: Tepoztlan Restudied*, University of Illinois Press, 1951.
8. R. Redfield, *Tepoztlan, A Mexican Village: A Study of Folk Life*. University of Chicago Press, 1930.
9. M. Avila, *Tradition and Growth*, University of Chicago Press, 1969.
10. R. Redfield, *The Primitive World and its Transformations*, Penguin, 1968, p. 158.
11. Burgess *op. cit.* (ch.3, n.4, ch.3, n.17 and ch.3, n.29).
12. J. R. Seeley, 'Crestwood Heights: intellectual and libidinal dimensions of research', in A. Vidich *et al.* (eds.) *Reflections on Community Studies*, Wiley, 1964, pp. 157–206.
13. M. R. Stein, 'The eclipse of community: some glances at the education of a sociologist', in Vidich *et al.*, *op. cit.*, pp. 207–32.
14. K. H. Wolff, 'Surrender and community study: the study of Loma', in Vidich *et al.*, *op. cit.*, pp. 233–64.
15. Ditton, *op. cit.* (ch.3, n.13).
16. J. Patrick, *A Glasgow Gang Observed*, Eyre-Methuen, 1973.
17. Humphreys, *op. cit.* (ch.2, n.3).
18. W. F. Whyte, *Street Corner Society*, University of Chicago Press, 1943.
19. Festinger, Riecken and Schachter, *op. cit.*

Controversy 6. What do school leavers think about schools?

1. P. Willis, *Learning to Labour*, Saxon House, 1978.
2. D. E. Scharff, 'Aspects of the transition from school to work', in J. M. M. Hill and D. E. Scharff, *Between Two Worlds*, Careers Consultants Ltd., 1976, pp. 66–332.
3. Willis, *op. cit.*, p. 11.
4. Scharff, *op. cit.*, pp. 235–54.
5. C. Griffin, *Typical Girls? The Transition from School to Unemployment for Young Working Class Women*, Routledge and Kegan Paul, 1986.

Chapter 6. Information through asking questions

1. R. Jowell and G. Hoinville, 'Opinion polls tested', *New Society*, 7 Aug. 1969, pp. 206–7.
2. R. Blackburn, 'A brief guide to bourgeois ideology', in A. Cockburn and R. Blackburn, *Student Power*, Penguin 1969, pp. 199–200.
3. N. Gross, W. S. Mason and A. W. McEachern, *Explorations in Role Analysis*, Wiley, 1966.
4. S. L. Payne, *The Art of Asking Questions*, Princeton University Press, 1951.

5.   J. Hagedorn, 'Students lack language skills' a report on research organised by J. Morris, *TES*, 8 Aug. 1986, p. 6.
6.   R. Knight, 'Don't go back to square one', *TES*, 22 Aug. 1986, p. 4. See also 'Testing techniques', letter to *TES*, 29 Aug. 1986, p. 12.
7.   A. Smithers and S. Carlisle, 'Reluctant teachers', *New Society*, 5 March 1970, pp. 391–2.
8.   M. D. Shipman 'Environmental influences on response to questionnaires', *Br. J. Ed. Psy.*, 1967.
9.   E. Z. Vogt and R. Hyman, *Water Witching U.S.A.*, University of Chicago Press, 1959, pp. 92–9.
10. Kinsey, *op. cit.* (ch.4, n.12).
11. Government Social Survey, *Handbook for Interviewers*, H.M.S.O.
12. C. A. Moser, *Survey Methods in Social Investigation*, Heinemann, 1958, pp. 193–4.
13. J. Durbin and A. Stuart, 'Differences in response rates of experienced and inexperienced interviewers', *J. Roy. Statistical Society*, 1951, pp. 163–205.
14. J. Rich, *Interviewing Children and Adolescents*, Macmillan, 1968.
15. J. Holt, 'Ask a silly question', *The TES*, 17 July 1970, p. 4.
16. P. Townsend, *The Last Refuge*, Routledge and Kegan Paul, 1962, pp. 3–16; see also P. Townsend, *The Family Life of Old People*, Routledge and Kegan Paul, 1956, pp. 3–10.
17. Kinsey, *op. cit.* (ch.4, n.12).
18. See N. K. Denzin, *op. cit.* (ch.3, n.30) pp. 122–43.
19. Newson and Newson, *op. cit.* (ch.4, n.20).

Controversy 7. To stream or unstream?

1.   J. C. Barker Lunn, *Streaming in the Primary School*, N.F.E.R., 1970.
2.   I. E. Finch, 'A study of the personal and social consequence of groups of secondary schooling of the experience of different methods of allocation within secondary courses', M.A. thesis, University of London, 1954.
3.   W. G. A. Rudd, 'The psychological effects of streaming by attainment with special reference to a group of selected children', *Br. J. Ed. Psy.*, 1956, pp. 47–60.
4.   J. S. Blandford, 'Standardised tests in junior schools with special reference to the effects of streaming on the consistency of results', *Br. J. Ed. Psy.*, 1958, pp. 170–3.
5.   J. M. Morris, *Reading in the Primary School*, N.F.E.R., 1959.
6.   J. C. Daniels, 'Some effects of segregation and streaming on the intellectual and scholastic development of Junior School children', Ph.D. thesis, University of Nottingham, 1959.
7.   A. Yates and D. A. Pidgeon, 'The effects of streaming', *Ed. Res.*, Nov. 1959.
8.   B. Simon, 'Non-streaming in the Junior School', *Forum*, 1964.
9.   Douglas, *op. cit.* (ch.3, n.8).
10. B. Jackson, *Streaming*, Routledge & Kegan Paul, 1964.
11. Barker Lunn, *op. cit.*
12. M. Goldberg et al., *Effects of Ability Grouping*, Columbia University Press, 1966.
13. R. B. Ekstrom, *Experimental Studies of Homogeneous Grouping: a review of the literature*, Princeton University Press, 1959.

14. See S. MacIure, *Education*, 2 May 1969.
15. A. Yates, *Grouping in Education*, Hamburg, Unesco Institute for Education, 1966, pp. 131-2. See also T. Husen, *International Study of Achievement in Mathematics*, Stockholm, Almquist & Wicksell, 1967.
16. Surrey Educational Research Association, *To Stream or not to Stream*, 1968.
17. J. Barker Lunn, 'Streaming in the Primary School', in M. Shipman, *The organisation and impact of social research*, Routledge and Kegan Paul, 1976, pp. 91-119.
18. M. Reid *et al.*, *Mixed Ability Teaching: Problems and Possibilities*, N.F.E.R./ Nelson, 1981.
19. K. Postlethwaite and C. Denton, *Streams for the Future*, Rubansco, 1978.
20. Y. Dar and N. Resh, *Classroom Composition and Pupil Achievement*, Gordon and Breach,1986.

Chapter 7. Experiments

1. Barker Lunn, *op. cit.* (Controversy 7, n.1).
2. C. Burstall, *French in the Primary School*, N.F.E.R.
3. Plowden Report, *Children and their Primary Schools*, H.M.S.O., 1967. See also, A. H. Halsey (ed.) *Educational Priority, volume 1*, H.M.S.O., 1972.
4. See Controversy 2.
5. F. J. Roethlisberger and W. J. Dickson, *Management and the Worker*, Wiley, 1939.
6. A. Carey, 'The Hawthorne Studies: a radical analysis',*Am. Soc. Rev.*, 1967, pp. 403-16.
7. R. Rosenthal, *Experimenter Effects in Behavioural Research*, Appleton-Century-Crofts, 1966.
8. R. Rosenthal and L. Jacobson,*Pygmalion in the Classroom*, Holt, Rinehart and Winston, 1968.
9. J. D. Elashoff and R. E. Snow, *Pygmalion Reconsidered*, Ç. A. Jones, 1971.
10. *Ibid.*, pp. 8-18. See also R. L. Thorndike, 'Review of Pygmalion in the Classroom', *American Education Research Journal* 5, 1968, pp. 708-11.
11. Elashoff and Snow, *op. cit.*
12. Thorndike, *op. cit.*
13. R. E. Snow, 'Unfinished Pygmalion', *Contemporary Psychology*, 14, 1969, pp. 197-9.
14. Elashoff and Snow,*op. cit.* See also R. Rosenthal, 'The Pygmalion effect lives', *Psychology Today*, 7, 4, 1973, pp. 56-63.
15. J. P. Barker and J. L. Crist, 'Teacher expectations: a review of the literature', in Elashoff and Snow, *op. cit.*, pp. 48-64.

Controversy 8. When was childhood discovered?

1. P. Ariès, *Centuries of Childhood*, J. Cape, 1962.
2. See J. Piaget, *The Psychology of Intelligence*, Routledge and Kegan Paul, 1947.
3. T. Parsons, *The Social System*, Free Press, 1951.
4. See, for example, M. Hoyles, 'Childhood in historical perspective', in M. Hoyes (ed.), *Changing Childhood*, Writers and Readers Coop., 1979, pp. 16-29. See also E. Shorter, *The Making of the Modern Family*, Collins, 1976.

5. J. Sommerville, *The Rise and Fall of Childhood*, Sage, 1982.
6. L. A. Pollock, *Forgotten Children*, Cambridge University Press, 1983.
7. L. de Mause, 'The evolution of childhood', in L. de Mause, *The History of Childhood*, Souvenir Press, 1976, pp. 1-74.
8. A. Wilson, 'The infancy of the history of childhod: an appraisal of Philippe Ariès, *History and Theory*, **19**, 1980, pp. 132-54.
9. J. B. Watson, *Psychological Care of Infant and Child*, Norton, 1928.
10. E. LeR. Ladurie, *Montaillou: Cathars and Catholics in a French Village, 1294-1324*, Scolar Press, 1978.
11. Pollock, *op. cit.*
12. F. Mount, *The Subversive Family*, J. Cape, 1982.
13. See M. D. Shipman, *Childhood*, N.F.E.R., 1972, pp. 46-7.

Chapter 8. Documents, unobtrusive measures and triangulation

1. A. V. Cicourel, *The Social Organization of Juvenile Justice*, Wiley, 1967.
2. W. I. Thomas and F. Znaniecki, *The Polish Peasant in Europe and America*, University of Chicago Press, 1918-20.
3. Blumer, *op. cit.* (ch.4, n.1), pp. 28-53.
4. *Ibid.*, pp. 74-6 and 109-10.
5. L. Gottschalk *et al.*, 'The use of personal documents in history', *Anthropology and Sociology*, 1951, pp. 3-75.
6. J. Dollard, *Criteria for the Life History*, Yale University Press, 1935.
7. J. Snodgrass, 'The Jack Roller at seventy: a fifty year follow-up of the delinquent boy's own story'. *Paper at the American Society of Criminology*, November, 1978.
8. E. H. Sutherland, *Professional Thief*, University of Chicago Press, 1966.
9. J. Snodgrass, 'The criminologist and his criminal: The case of Erwin H. Sutherland and Broadway Jones', *Issues in Criminology*, **8**,1, pp. 1-17, 1973.
10. See K. Plummer, *Documents of Life*, Allen and Unwin, 1983.
11. I. Goodson, *School Subjects and Curriculum Change*, Croom Helm, 1982.
12. Home Office, *Report of the Departmental Committee on Criminal Statistics*, Cmnd. 3448, 1967.
13. Home Office, *op. cit.*, pp. 10-11.
14. J. Irvine, I. Miles and J. Evans, *Demystifying Social Statistics*, Pluto Press, 1981.
15. E. J. Webb *et al.*, *Unobtrusive Measures*, Rand McNally, 1966.
16. K. Plummer, *op. cit.*, p. 87.
17. N. K. Denzin, *op. cit.* (ch.3, n.30).
18. R. G. Burgess, *op. cit.* (ch.3, n.8).

Controversy 9. How could psychology include fraud? The case of Sir Cyril Burt

1. K. Pearson, *The Life, Letters and Labours of Francis Galton*, Vol.2, Cambridge University Press, 1924.
2. L. S. Hearnshaw, *Cyril Burt: Psychologist*, Hodder and Stoughton, 1979.

3. *Ibid.*
4. L. J. Kamin, *The Science and Politics of IQ*, Erlbaum, 1974.
5. O. Gillie, 'Crucial data was faked by eminent psychologist', *Sunday Times*, 24 Oct. 1976.
6. A. D. B. and A. M. Clarke, *Mental Deficiency*, 3rd edn, Methuen, 1974.

Chapter 9. The author, the date and the context

1. H. Roberts, *op. cit.* (ch.2, n.13).
2. L. Stanley and S. Wise, *op. cit.* (ch.2, n.14).
3. D. Spender, *Invisible Women*, Writers and Readers, 1982.
4. R. R. Dale, *Mixed or Single-Sex School?* Routledge and Kegan Paul, 1969.
5. J. W. B. Douglas, *The Home and the School*, McGibbon and Kee, 1964.
6. C. Lacey, 'Problems of sociological fieldwork: a review of the methodology of "Hightown Grammar" ', in M. D. Shipman, *The Organisation and Impact of Social Research*, Routledge and Kegan Paul, 1976, pp. 63–88.
7. A. V. Gouldner, 'Anti-Minotaur: the myth of value-free sociology', *Social Problems*, **9**, 1962, pp. 199–213.
8. C. W. Mills, *The Sociological Imagination*, Oxford University Press, 1959, pp. 50–75.
9. W. G. Runciman, 'Thinking by Numbers', *TES*, 6 Aug. 1971, pp. 943–4.
10. F. J. Roethlisberger and W. J. Dickson, *Management and the Worker*, Wiley, 1939.
11. R. Lippitt and R. K. White, 'An experimental study of leadership and group life', in H. P. Proshansky and B. Seidenberg, *Basic Studies in Social Psychology*, Holt, Rinehart and Winston, 1965, pp. 523–37.
12. B. R. McCandless, *Children, Behaviour and Development*, Holt, Rinehart and Winston, 1967, p. 564.
13. J. Platt, *The Realities of Research*, University of Sussex Press, 1976.
14. Bell and Newby, *op. cit.* (ch.3, n.20).
15. Shipman, *op. cit.* (n.6 above).
16. Burgess *op. cit.* (ch.5, n.11).
17. R. R. Dale, ' "Mixed or single-sex school": a comment on a research study', in M. D. Shipman, *op. cit.* (n.6), pp. 120–38.
18. J. and E. Newson, 'Parental roles and social contexts', in M. D. Shipman *ibid.*, pp. 22–48.
19. C. Bell, 'Reflections on the Banbury Restudy', in Bell and Newby, *op. cit.* (ch.3, n.20), pp. 47–107.
20. J. Ford, 'Facts, evidence and rumour: a rational reconstruction of "Social Class and the Comprehensive School" ', in Shipman, *op. cit.* (n.6), pp. 51–62.
21. J. W. B. Douglas, 'The use and abuse of national cohorts', in Shipman, *ibid.*, pp. 3–21.
22. Dale, *op. cit.* p. 121.
23. H. Becker, 'Problems in the publication of field studies', in J. Bynner and K. M. Stribley, *Social Research: Principles and Procedures*, Longman, 1978.
24. J. G. Goldthorpe, *op. cit.* (ch.4, n.22) and A. H. Halsey *et al.*, *Origins and Destinations*, Clarendon Press, 1980.
25. D. H. Hargreaves, *op. cit.* (ch.3, n.5).
26. C. Lacey, *op. cit.* (ch.3, n.6).
27. C. Lacey, 'Some sociological concomitants of academic streaming in a grammar school', *Br. J. Soc.*, **18**, 1966, pp. 245–62.

188   *The Limitations of Social Research*

28. C. Mullard, 'Multiracial education in Britain: From assimilation to cultural pluralism', in J. Tierney (ed.), *Race, Migration and Schooling*, Holt, Rinehart and Winston, 1982, pp. 120–33.
29. Plowden Report, *op. cit.* (ch.7, n.3).
30. Inner London Education Authority, *Race, Sex and Class, 2. Multi-Ethnic Education in Schools*, I.L.E.A., 1983.
31. M. Mead, *Blackberry Winter*, Angus and Robertson, 1972.
32. F. Coffield, *op. cit.* (ch.4, n.10).
33. I. L. Horowitz, *The Rise and Fall of Project Camelot*, Massachusetts Institute of Technology Press, 1967; see also G. Sjoberg, *Ethics, Politics and Social Research*, Routledge & Kegan Paul, 1969, pp. 141–61.
34. W. O. Hagstrom, *The Scientific Community*, Basic Books, 1965, pp. 69–104.
35. R. K. Merton, 'Priorities in scientific discovery', in B. Barber and W. Hirsch, *The Sociology of Science*, Free Press, 1962, pp. 447–85.
36. I. L. Horowitz, 'The natural history of "Revolution in Brazil"; a biography of a book', in Sjoberg, *op. cit.* pp. 198–224.
37. J. Ford, *Social Class and the Comprehensive School*, Routledge & Kegan Paul, 1969, pp. vii and viii.
38. Z. A. Medvedev, *The Rise and Fall of T. D. Lysenko*, Columbia University Press, 1969.
39. See *TES*, 7 Aug. 1970, p. 1 and *TES*, 21 Aug. 1970, p. 10.
40. J. D. Watson, *The Double Helix*, Weidenfeld & Nicolson, 1968.
41. J. S. Weiner, *The Piltdown Forgery*, Oxford University Press, 1955.
42. D. S. Greenberg, *The Politics of American Science*, Penguin, 1969, pp. 219–60.

Controversy 10. The Swann Report and the politics of research

1. Inner London Education Authority, *Literacy Survey: 1971 follow-up preliminary report*, I.L.E.A., RS 567A/72, 1972.
2. M. Swann, *Education for All*, H.M.S.O., 1985.
3. *Education*, 'Swann: Controversy mars report's publication', 15 March 1985, p. 1.
4. *TES*, 'Final row for troubled Swann', 15 March 1985, p. 1.
5. *TES*, 'Sir Keith moves quickly to kill key Swann recommendation', 22 March 1986, p. 6.
6. National Anti-Racist Movement in Education, *NAME on Swann*, NAME, 1985.
7. Commission for Racial Equality, *Swann*, C.R.E., 1985.
8. Runnymeade Trust, *Education for All*, Runnymeade Trust, 1985.

Chapter 10. The publication of research

1. Rutter *op. cit.* (ch.2, n.4).
2. Goldstein *op. cit.* (ch.2, n.9).
3. S. Labovitz, 'The nonutility of significance tests: the significance of tests of significance reconsidered', *Pacific Sociological Review*, 1970, pp. 141–8.
4. See, for example, Radical Statistics Education Group, *op. cit.* (ch.2, n.7).
5. P. L. Freeman, title as in text, *Br. Ed. Res. J.*, 12 Feb. 1986, pp. 197–206.

6. P. Mitchell, 'A teacher's view of educational research', in M. Shipman, *op. cit.* (ch.2, n.19), pp. 81–96.
7. D. H. Drysdale, 'Research and the education administrator', in M. Shipman *ibid.*, pp. 72–80.
8. See, for example, J. Nixon, *A Teacher's Guide to Action Research*, Grant McIntyre, 1981.
9. J. W. N. Watkins, 'Confession is good for ideas', in D. Edge (ed.), *Experiment*, B.B.C., 1964, pp. 64–70.
10. M. T. Oldcom, 'The ABC's of groupness', *J. Abnormal Psychology*, **5**, pp. 6–45.
11. W. Taylor, 'The school's task and the teacher's task', in Department of Education and Science, *Better Schools: Evaluation and Appraisal Conference*, H.M.S.O., 1986, p. 25.
12. J. W. Wiggins and H. Schoeck, 'A profile of the aged: U.S.A.', *Geriatrics*, July, 1961, pp. 336–42.
13. L. D. Cain, 'The AMA and the gerontologists: uses and abuses of "A profile of the aged: U.S.A." ', in G. Sjoberg, *Ethics, Politics and Social Research*, Routledge and Kegan Paul, 1969, pp. 78–114.
14. J. W. Wiggins and H. Schoeck, *Scientism and Values*, Van Nostrand, 1960.
15. S. N. Bennett, *Teaching Styles and Pupil Progress*, Open Books, 1976. For criticism see J. Gray and D. Satterley, 'A chapter of errors: teaching styles and pupil progress in retrospect', *Educational Research*, **19**,3, 1976, pp. 45–56. See also Controversy 11.
16. J. S. Coleman, *op. cit.* (ch.2, n.2).
17. H. R. Alker, 'A typology of ecological fallacies', in M. Dogan and S. Rokkan, *Quantitative Ecological Analysis in the Social Sciences*, M.I.T. Press, 1969.
18. M. W. Riley, *Sociological Research*, Harcourt, Brace and World, 1963, pp. 700–9.
19. P. Willis, *Learning to Labour*, Saxon House, 1978.
20. P. Willis, *Profane Culture*, Routledge and Kegan Paul, 1978.
21. F. Musgrove, 'Review of "Profane Culture" ', *Research in Education*, **20**, 1979, pp. 93–6.
22. D. Riesman, *The Lonely Crowd*, Doubleday, 1953.
23. E. Larrabee, 'David Riesman and his readers', in S. M. Lipset and L. Lownethal, *Character and Social Structure*, Free Press, 1961.
24. D. Riesman and N. Glazer, 'A reconsideration', in Lipset and Lowenthal, *ibid.*, pp. 419–58.
25. R. Wild, 'The background to *Bradstow*: reflections and reactions' in C. Bell and S. Encel, *Inside the Whale*, Pergamon, 1978.
26. J. Ford, 'Facts, evidence and rumour', in Shipman, *op. cit.* (ch.9, n.6).
27. J. Barker Lunn *op. cit.* (cont. 7., n.17).
28. J. A. Downing, *The i.t.a. Reading Experiment*, Evans, 1964.
29. F. W. Warburton and V. Southgate, *i.t.a.: An Independent Evaluation*, Murray and Chambers, 1969.
30. D. Moyle, *The Teaching of Reading*, Ward Lock, 1968, p. 83.
31. S. Isaacs, *Social Development in Young Children*, Routledge, 1933.
32. J. Piaget, *The Language and Thought of the Child*, Kegan Paul, 1926.
33. P. Bryant, 'Piaget, teachers and psychology', *Oxford Rev. of Ed.*, **10**,3, 1984, pp. 251–9.
34. Plowden Report, *Children and their Primary Schools*, H.M.S.O., 1967, p. 142.
35. See, for example, T. G. R. Bower, *The Preceptual World of the Child*, Fontana, 1977.
36. M. Donaldson, *Children's Minds*, Fontana/Collins, 1978.

37. P. E. Bryant and T. Trabasso, 'Transitive inferences and memory in young children', *Nature*, **232**, 1971, 456–8.
38. *Observer*, 22 Aug. 1 971, p. 4 and 12 Sept. 1971, p. 7.
39. *Daily Telegraph*, 23 Aug. 1971, p. 3.
40. *Observer*, 12 Sept. 1971, p. 7.
41. J. H. Flavell, *The Developmental Psychology of Jean Piaget*, Van Nostrand, 1963.
42. B. J. Wadsworth, *Piaget's Theory of Cognitive Development*, Longman, 1976.
43. National Froebel Foundation, *Some Aspects of Piaget's Work*, National Froebel Foundation, 1955.
44. E. M. Churchill, *Piaget's Findings and the Teacher*, National Froebel Foundation, 1960/61.
45. N. Isaacs, *A Brief Introduction to Piaget*, Agathan Press, 1972, first published in 1961.
46. N. Isaacs, *Piaget: Some Answers to Teachers' Questions*, National Froebel Foundation, 1965.
47. M. Brearley and E. Hitchfield, *A Teacher's Guide to Reading Piaget*, Routledge and Kegan Paul, 1966.
48. R. M. Beard, *An Outline of Piaget's Developmental Psychology for Students and Teachers*, Basic Books, 1969.
49. D. G. Boyle, *A Student's Guide to Piaget*, Pergamon, 1969.
50. H. G. Furth, *Piaget for Teachers*, Prentice Hall, 1970.
51. M. Schwebel, *Piaget in the Classroom*, Basic Books, 1973.
52. S. F. Campbell, *Piaget Sampler*, Wiley, 1976.
53. M. Hardeman, *Children's Ways of Knowing: Nathan Isaacs on Education, Psychology and Piaget*, New York, Teachers College Press, 1974.

Controversy 11. Do teaching styles affect pupil progress?

1. S. N. Bennett, *Teaching Styles and Pupil Progress*, Open Books, 1976.
2. *TES*, 30 April 1976, pp. 19–22.
3. See G. Bernbaum (ed.), *Schooling in Decline*, Macmillan, 1979.
4. *TES*, 7 May 1976, p. 14.
5. G. W. Miller, letter to *TES*, 14 May 1976, p. 15.
6. D. McIntyre, review of Bennett (above, n.1) in *Br. J. of Teacher Education*, **2** (3), 1977, pp. 291–7.
7. *TES*, 30 April 1976, pp. 19–22.
8. *Ibid.*, p. 3.
9. J. Gray, 'What really goes on in class', in *TES*, 7 May 1976, p. 24.
10. R. Sinha, letter to *TES*, 7 May 1976, p. 24.
11. A. Clegg, letter to *TES*, 14 May 1976, p. 15.
12. E. de Bono, letter to *TES*, 14 May 1976, p. 15.
13. S. N. Bennett and N. Entwistle, 'Informal or formal: a reply', *TES*, 21 May 1976, p. 2.
14. R. Walker, letter to *TES*, 28 May 1976, p. 20.
15. J. M. Hughes, letter to *TES*, 28 May 1976, p. 20.
16. *TES*, 4 June 1976, pp. 17–19.
17. J. Gray, letter to *TES*, 4 June 1976, p. 8.
18. J. Bruner, 'The styles of teaching', in *New Society*, 29 April 1976, pp. 223–5.
19. D. Satterly, letter to *New Society*, 6 May 1976, p. 315.

20. J. Gray and D. Satterly, 'A chapter of errors: teaching styles and pupil progress in retrospect', in *Ed. Res.* **19**, 1976, pp. 45–56.
21. S. N. Bennett and N. Entwistle, 'Rite and Wrong: a reply to "A Chapter of Errors",' in *Ed. Res.* **19**, 1976, pp. 217–22.
22. *Harvard Ed. Rev.* **47** (2), 1977, pp. 214–21.
23. M. Aitkin *et al.*, 'Teaching styles and pupil progress: a Re-analysis', in *Br. J. Ed. Psy.*, **51**, 1981, pp. 170–86.
24. J. Hesketh, 'When best is not good enough', in *TES*, 17 May 1981, p. 15.
25. M. Galton and B. Simon, *Progress and Performance in the Primary Classroom*, Routledge and Kegan Paul, 1980.
26. R. Barrow, *op. cit.* (ch.3, n.35).
27. *Ibid.*
28. N. Bennett *et al.*, *The Quality of Pupils Learning Experiences*, Erlbaum, 1984.

Chapter 11. The scope and limitations of social research

1. Bell and Encel, *op. cit.* (ch.10, n.25).
2. G. H. Bantock, 'Literature and the social sciences', paper read at the Annual Conference of the British Sociological Association, 1970.
3. M. V. Harrold and M. H. Temple, 'A study of children in the admission classes of four infant schools', in W. van der Eyken, *The Pre-School Years*, Penguin, 1967, pp. 102–11.
4. J. E. Mears, 'Unleashing the untrained: some observations of student ethnographers', *Human Organization*, Summer, 1969, pp. 155–60.
5. See, for example, G. Myrdal, *The Political Element in the Development of Economic Thought*, Routledge and Kegan Paul, 1953.
6. Medawar, *op. cit.* (ch.1, n.4).
7. M. Kogan, *Government's Commissioning of Research*, Brunel University, 1980.
8. C. Weiss, 'The many meanings of research utilization', *Public Administration Review*, 9 Oct. 1979, pp. 426–31. See also C. Weiss, 'Policy research in the context of diffuse decision making', in D. B. P. Kallen *et al.*, *Social Science Research and Public Policy-Making*, N.F.E.R.-Nelson, 1982, pp. 288–321.
9. Bennett, *op. cit.* (ch.10, n.15).
10. Rutter, *op. cit.* (ch.2, n.4).
11. J. W. Campbell, 'Rocket flight to the moon', *Philosophical Magazine*, Jan. 1941.
12. See A. C. Clarke, *Profiles of the Future*, Pan, 1973, p. 26.
13. E. Charles, 'The effect of present trends in fertility and morality upon the future population of Great Britain and upon its age composition', in L. Hogben, *Political Arithmetic*, Allen and Unwin, 1938, pp. 73–105.
14. E. H. Erikson, *Childhood and Society*, Norton, 1950.
15. A. R. Jensen, 'How much can we boost IQ and scholastic achievement?', *Harvard Ed. Rev.*, Winter, 1969, pp. 1–123.
16. *Harvard Ed. Rev.*, Spring 1969.
17. W. F. Brazziel, 'A letter from the South', *Harvard Ed. Rev.*, Spring 1969, p. 348.
18. *Ibid.*
19. M. K. Barry, letter to *New Society*, 24 June 1971, p. 1108.
20. A. R. Jensen, 'Do schools cheat minority children?', *Ed. Res.*, **14**,1, 1971, pp. 3–28.

21. M. Morris, quoted in B. Hill, 'N.F.E.R. attacked over Jensen article', *TES*, 17 Sept. 1971, p. 5.
22. D. Pidgeon, quoted in Hill, *ibid.*
23. H. J. Eysenck, *Race, Intelligence and Education*, M. Temple Smith, 1971.
24. See *New Society*, 24 June 1971 and 1 July 1971, pp. 29–30.
25. W. F. Bodmer and L. L. Cavalli-Sforza, 'Intelligence and race', *Scientific American*, 10/1970, pp. 19–29.
26. W. Bodmer, 'Genetics and intelligence: the race argument', in Halsey *op. cit.* (cont. 1, n.4), p. 319.
27. H. Eysenck and S. Rose, 'Race, intelligence and education', *New Community*, 7,2, 1979, pp. 278–83.
28. N. J. Block and G. Dworkin, 'IQ, heritability and inequality', in Block and Dworkin *op. cit.* (ch.1, n.3), pp. 410–540.
29. Block and Dworkin, *ibid.*
30. R. K. Merton, *Social Theory and Social Structure*, Free Press, 1957.
31. P. Woods, 'Having a laugh: an antidote to schooling', in M. Hammersley and P. Woods (eds.), *The Process of Schooling*, Routledge and Kegan Paul, 1979, pp. 178–187.
32. R. King, *op. cit.* (ch.3, n.21).
33. J. Rex, *Sociology, the Demystification of the Modern World*, Routledge and Kegan Paul, 1975.

INDEX

Aitkin, M., 158-9
Alker, H.R., 146
Ariès, P., 102, 103
Authoritarian Personality, 61-2
Avila, M., 71

Bales, R.F., 70
Ball, S., 39
Bantock, G.H., 162-3
Barker Lunn, J., 92, 96, 148
Barrow, R., 46
Becker, H., 126
Bell, C., 44
Bennett, S.N., 16, 17, 49, 145,
    155-60, 168
bias, 164-5
Blackburn, R., 79-80
Blandford, J.S., 90
Block, N.J., 174
Blandot, Blondlot or Blondot, R. or
    P. or M., 9-10, 69-70
Boas, F., 3, 32
Bodmer, W.F., 173
Boyson, R., 156
Brazziel, W.F., 172
British Educational Research
    Association, 49
British Institute of Public Opinion,
    86
Bruner, J., 156, 157
Bryant, P.E., 151, 152, 153
Bullock Report, 60, 61
Burgess, R.B., 39, 56, 71, 115, 126
Burstall, C., 96
Burt, C., 119-121, 122, 128

Campbell, J.W., 169

Cavalli-Sforza, L.L., 173
census, 54, 87, 108
Centre for Educational Sociology, 18
Charles, E., 169
Chicago School of Sociology, 21, 27
Cicourel, A.V., 109
Clarke, A.D.B., 121
Clarke, A.M., 121
Clarke, J. 65, 66
Clegg, A., 156
Clever Hans, 84
Coffield, F., 130
Coleman, J.S., 15, 145, 174
Commission for Racial Equality, 138
Comte, A., 28, 170
control, 94-6
Conwell, C., 111
correlational research 97
Cottrell, A., 6
Cox, C., 48, 49, 50, 51
Crick, F.H.C., 134

Dale, R.R., 122, 126
Dalton, J., 6
Dancy, J., 49
Daniels, J.C., 90, 92
Dar, Y., 93
Darwin, C., 2, 19, 32, 119, 120
Davies, L., 70
Dawson, C., 135
de Bono, E., 156
Delamont, S., 42, 43
DeMause, L., 103
Department of Education and
    Science, 1, 48, 50, 155
    Assessment of Performance Unit,
    55, 61, 171-2

determinism, 19–20, 24, 33, 35,
  170–1
  biological, 2–4, 32–6
  cultural, 3–4, 32–6
Ditton, J., 39, 72
documents, 107–115
Dollard, J., 111
Donaldson, M., 152
Douglas, J.W.B., 23, 60, 91, 92, 122,
  126
Drysdale, D.H., 142
Durbin, J., 86
Durkheim, E., 27, 128
Dworkin, G., 174

Economic and Social Research
  Council, 7
Elashoff, J.D., 100
Entwhistle, H., 156, 157
ethogenicism, 21
ethnography, 27–8, 37–46
Erikson, E.H., 170
experiment, 30, 94–101
  ex post facto, 94, 96
  quasi, 94, 96
experimental effects, 97–101
Eugenics Record Office, 3
evaluation, 96–7
Eysenck, H., 173, 174

fallacies, 146
feminist research, 25, 122–3
Festinger, I., 73
Fielding, N., 39
Finch, I.F., 90
Flew, A., 50
Floud, J., 23
Fode, K.L., 69
Fogelman, K., 23, 49
Ford, J., 132, 148
Freeman, D., 34
Freud, S., 19, 32, 35, 36, 151, 170,
  171
functionalism, 28, 33, 162

Gabriel, J., 60
Galton, F., 32, 119, 120
Galton, M., 42, 43, 159
General Household Survey, 60
generalisability, iii, 53–62
Giddens, A., 27
Gillie, O., 120

Glaser, B., 41
Glass, D., 23
Glazer, N., 147
Goldstein, H., 16–17, 140
Goldthorpe, J.H., 60
Goodson, I., 112
Gottschalk, L., 110
Gouldner, A.V., 124
Government Social Survey, 62, 79,
  85–6
Gray, J., 49, 50, 156
Griffin, C., 77
Guzzetti, B.J., 144–5

Hagstrom, W.O., 131
Halfpenny, D., 38
Hall, G.S., 32, 33, 35, 36
Hall, S., 65
Halsey, A.H., 23
Hammersley, M., 40, 42
Hargreaves, D.H., 39, 57, 128
Harré, R., 45
Harrold, M.V., 163–4
Harvard Educational Review, 157
Hawthorne effect, 98, 125
Hearnshaw, L.S., 119, 120, 121
Heath, A.F., 23
Hemming, J., 58
Henry, S., 39
Her Majesty's Inspectors, 55–6
Hesketh, J., 159
Hitler, A., 2, 108, 119, 125
Hoinville, G., 78
Holt, J., 86–7
Homan, R., 39, 70
Horowitz, I.L., 132
Howell, D., 64
Huberman, M., 134
Hughes, J.M., 156
Humphreys, L., 22, 39, 72

initial teaching alphabet, 149
Inner London Education Authority,
  17, 51, 130, 138
interviews, 84–9
Isaacs, S., 150–1

Jackson, B., 91
Jacobson, L., 99–101
Jencks, C., 15
Jenkins, D., 40
Jensen, A.R., 172, 173, 174

Jones, B., 50
Joseph, K., 7, 12, 50, 138
Jowell, R., 78

Kamin, L.J., 120
King, G., 169
King, R., 175
Kinsey, A.C., 58, 84–5, 87–8
Kogan, M., 166
Krushchev, N., 132, 133
Kuhn, T.S., 11, 12

Lacey, C., 39, 124, 127, 128
Ladurie, E. LeR., 104
Lewin, K., 125
Lewis, O., 71
life history, 21
Lindsay, K., 23
Lippitt, R., 125
Lysenko, T.D., 132, 133, 144

McCaghy, C.H., 29, 38
McCarthy, J., 133
McDougall, W., 2
McIntyre, D., 156
McNamara, D., 42
Maine, H., 170
Malinowski, B., 38
Marks, J., 48, 49, 50, 51
Marsh, P., 45, 66, 156
Marx, K., 19, 128, 162, 171
Mass Observation, 21
Mayo, E., 98
Mead, G.H., 27
Mead, M., 3, 32–6, 130
Medawar, P., 10, 166
Merton, R.K., 131, 175
Miller, G.W., 155
Mills, C.W., 124
Mitchell, P., 142
models, 8–11, 21, 28, 161–2
Morris, J.M., 81–2, 90
Mortimore, P., 16, 17, 51
Mount, F., 105
Musgrove, F., 60, 147

National Association for
    Multi-Cultural Education, 138
National Children's Bureau, 48, 49
National Child Development
    Survey, 48
National Foundation for Educational

Research, 9
Newby, H., 29, 1.
Newcomb, S., 12
Newson, E., 60, 88–
Newson, J., 60, 88–9
Norwood Report, 128

observation, 37–46, 68–
    participative, 37, 71–3
Office of Population Censuses and
    Surveys, 61
Oldcom, M.T., 144
ORACLE, 42–4, 46, 56, 70, 159
Owen, J., 156

Parsons, T., 33, 35, 103
Patrick, J., 72
Payne, S.L., 81
Pearson, K., 2
Pfungst, P.O., 84
Piaget, J., 102, 151–4, 170
Pidgeon, D.A., 90
pilot studies, 80
Piltdown Man, 135, 168–9
Pitman, I., 149
Pitman, J., 149
Plowden Report, 90, 91, 96, 129,
    130, 151, 152
Pollock, L.A., 103, 105
Pomian-Srzednicki, B., 49, 50, 51
Popper, K., 11, 12, 148
Porter, M.A., 41
positivism, 28
Powell, E., 79
Project Camelot, 131
Project Mohole, 136
publication, 127–30, 131–2, 139–154,
    174
Pygmalion effects, 99–101

questionnaires, 78–83

Rampton, A., 137
Rand Corporation, 15
Redfield, R., 71
reliability, ii, 26, 35, 38, 43, 46, 89,
    101, 109, 158, 163–4
Resh, N., 93
Rex, J., 176
Rich, J., 86
Ridge, J.M., 23
Riecken, H.W., 73

...sman, D., 147
Riley, M.W., 146
Röntgen, C.W., 9
Rose, S., 174
Rosenthal, R., 69, 99–101
Rosser, E., 45
Rudd, W.G.A., 90
Runciman, G., 124
Runnymede Trust, 138
Rutter, M., 16, 17, 49, 97, 140, 168

sampling, 52–63
    probability, 54, 55–6, 62
    purposive, 53, 54, 56–9, 62
    quota, 53, 54, 57–8, 62
    response, 59–62
    theoretical, 63
Satterley, D., 73
Schacter, S., 73
Scharff, S., D., 74–7
Schoeck, H., 145
scientific communities, 8, 9, 13
scientism, 6, 22, 31
Scottish Educational Data Archive,
    18
Shaw, C., 111
Shipman, M.D., 126
Simon, B., 159
Skipper, J.K., 29, 38
Snodgrass, J., 111
Snow, R.E., 100
social interaction, 21, 31
social phenomenology, 21, 26
Social Science Research Council, 7,
    12, 38, 66, 77, 162
Southgate, V., 29, 149
Spencer, H., 70, 171
Stacey, M., 44
Stalin, J., 132
Steedman, J., 49
Stein, M.R., 72
Stierer, B., 29
Strauss, A., 41
Summerville, J., 103
Sutherland, E.H., 111, 112

Swann Report, 129, 130, 137–8

Taylor, I., 65, 66
Taylor, W., 144–5
Temple, M.H., 163–4
Theory, 8–11, 161–2, 175
    grounded, 41, 63
Thomas, W.I., 51, 109–11
Thorndike, E.L., 100
Trabasso, T., 152, 153
triangulation, 43, 114–5
Turner, G., 41

unobtrusive measures, 113–5
Ussher, J., 170

validity, ii, 26, 38, 46, 89, 109, 158,
    167
Van Osten, 95–6
Vavilov, N.I., 132

Walker, R., 156
Wallace, G., 172
Wallis, R., 39, 40
Warburton, F., 149
Warnock Report, 60, 61
Watkins, J.W.N., 143
Watson, J.B., 104
Watson, J.D., 134
Webb, E.J., 114
Weiss, C., 166–7
White, R.K., 125
Whyte, W.F., 72
Wiggins, J.W.W., 145
Wild, R., 147–8
Willis, P., 74–77, 146, 175–6
Wilson, A., 104
Wolf, K.H., 72
Wood, R., 69
Woods, P., 40, 175
Wrigley, J., 50

Yates, A., 90

Znaniecki, F., 109–111